Messy
Spirituality

Christianity for the rest of us

MIKE YACONELLI

Hodder & Stoughton
LONDON SYDNEY AUCKLAND

Copyright © 2001 by Michael Yaconelli

First published in Great Britain in 2001

The right of Michael Yaconelli to be identified as the
Author of the Work has been asserted by him in accordance
with the Copyright, Designs and Patents Act 1988.

10 9 8 7 6 5 4 3 2 1

British Library Cataloguing in Publication Data
A record for this book is available from the British Library

ISBN 0 340 756635 7

Typeset by Avon Dataset Ltd, Bidford-on-Avon, Warks

Printed and bound in Great Britain by
The Guernsey Press Co. Ltd, Channel Isles

Hodder & Stoughton
A Division of Hodder Headline Ltd
338 Euston Road
London NW1 3BH

Messy
Spirituality

This is for my mom, Margaret Yaconelli,
who instilled in me a fondness for grace.

Contents

Messy

The workshop of the spiritual life

I stake the future on the few humble and hearty lovers who seek God passionately in the marvellous, messy world of redeemed and related realities that lie in front of our noses.

William McNamara[1]

Dear God,
I'm doing the best I can.

Frank[2]

I go into churches and everyone seems to feel so good about themselves. Everyone calls themselves a Christian nowadays. How dare we call ourselves Christians? It's only for Jesus to decide whether we are Christian or not. I don't think he's made a decision in my case, and I'm afraid that when he does I am going to be sent straight to hell. I don't feel I can call myself a Christian. I can't be satisfied with myself. We all seem to be pretty contented with ourselves in church and that makes me sick. I think all this contentment makes Jesus nervous.

Robert Coles[3]

My life is a mess.

After forty-five years of trying to follow Jesus, I keep losing him in the crowded busyness of my life. I know Jesus is there, somewhere, but it's difficult to make him out in the haze of everyday life.

For as long as I can remember I have wanted to be a godly person. Yet when I look at the yesterdays of my life, what I see, mostly, is the broken, irregular map of my past, littered with mistakes and failure. I have had temporary successes and isolated moments of closeness to God, but I long for the continuing presence of Jesus moment by moment. Most of the moments of my life seem hopelessly stuck in a tangled web of obligations and distractions.

I want to be a good person. I don't want to fail. I want to learn from my mistakes, rid myself of the distractions and run into the arms of Jesus. Most of the time, however, I feel as if I am running away from Jesus into the arms of my own cluttered-ness.

I want desperately to know God better. I want to be consistent. Right now the only consistency in my life is my inconsistency. Who I want to be and who I am are not very close together. I am not doing well at the living-a-consistent-life thing.

I don't want to be St John of the Cross or Billy

Graham, I just want to be remembered as a person who loved God, who served others more than he served himself, and a person who was trying to grow in maturity and stability. I want to have more victories than defeats, yet here I am, almost sixty, and I find myself failing on a regular basis.

If I were to die today, I would be nervous about what people would say at my eulogy. I would be happy if they said things like 'He was a nice guy' or 'He was occasionally decent' or 'Mike wasn't as bad as a lot of people.' Unfortunately, eulogies are delivered by people who know the deceased. I know what the unanimous consensus would be: 'Mike was a mess.'

When I was younger I believed my inconsistency was due to my youth. I believed age would teach me all I needed to know, and when I was older I would have learned the lessons of life and discovered the secrets of true spirituality.

I *am* older, a lot older, and I haven't learned very much. The secrets are still secret from me.

I often have a dream that I am tagging along behind Jesus, longing for him to choose me as one of his disciples. Without warning he turns around, looks straight into my eyes and says, 'Follow me!' My heart races and I am beginning to run towards him when he interrupts with, 'Oh, not you, the guy behind you. Sorry.'

I have been trying to follow Christ most of my life, and the best I can do is a stumbling, bumbling, clumsy kind of following. I wake up most days with the humiliating awareness that I have no clue where Jesus is. Even though I am a minister, even though I think about Jesus every day, my following is . . . uh . . . meandering.

So I've decided to write a book about the spiritual life.

I know what you're thinking. Based on what I've just said about my own walk with God, having me write about spirituality is like having Bozo the clown explain the meaning of the universe, like playing Handel's *Messiah* on the kazoo. How can someone whose life is obviously *un-spiritual* presume to talk about spirituality? How can someone un-holy presume to talk about holiness? It makes no sense.

Unless. Un*less!* Unless spirituality as most of us understand it is not spirituality at all.

Sadly, 'spiritual' has most commonly come to mean people who pray all day long, read their Bibles constantly, never get angry or rattled, possess special powers and have the inside track to God. Spirituality, for most, has an *other*-worldly ring to it, describing odd, eccentric 'saints' who have forsaken the ordinary world, taken a vow of poverty, isolated themselves in cloisters and hide in walled or distant retreat centres.

Nothing wrong with the spirituality of monks. They certainly experience a *kind* of spirituality, a way of seeking and knowing God – but *what about the rest of us?* What about those of us who live in the city, have a wife/ husband and three children, two cats and a washing machine that has stopped working? What about those of us who are single, work sixty to seventy hours a week, with parents who wonder why we're not married and friends who make much more money than we do? What about those of us who are divorced, still trying to heal from the scars of rejection, trying to cope with the single parenting of children who don't understand why this has happened to them?

Is there a spirituality for the rest of us who are not secluded in a monastery, who don't have it all together and probably never will?

The answer is yes!

What landed Jesus on the cross was the preposterous idea that common, ordinary, broken, screwed-up people *could be godly!* What drove Jesus' enemies crazy was his criticism of the 'perfect' religious people and his acceptance of the imperfect non-religious people. The shocking implication of Jesus' ministry is that *anyone* can be spiritual.

Scandalous? Maybe.

Maybe Truth *is* scandalous. Maybe the scandal is that all of us are in some condition of not-togetherness, even those of us who are trying to be godly. Maybe we're all a mess – not only sinful messy, but inconsistent messy, up-and-down messy, in-and-out messy, now-I-believe-now-I-don't messy, I-get-it-now-I-don't-get-it messy, I-understand-uh-now-I-don't-understand messy.

I admit, messy spirituality sounds ... well ... un-*spiritual.*

Surely there are guidelines to follow, principles to live by, maps to show us where to go and secrets we can uncover to discover a spirituality that is clean and tidy?

I'm afraid not.

Spirituality is not a formula, it is not a test, it is a relationship. Spirituality is not about competency, it is about intimacy. Spirituality is not about perfection, it is about connection. The way of the spiritual life begins where we are *now* in the mess of our lives. Accepting the reality of our broken flawed lives is the beginning of spirituality, not because the spiritual life will remove our flaws but because we *let go* of seeking perfection and, instead, seek God, the One who is present in the tangled-ness of our lives. Spirituality is not about being fixed, it is about God being present in the mess of our unfixedness.

Look at the Bible. Its pages overflow with messy people. The biblical writers didn't edit out the flaws of its heroes – like Noah, for example. Everyone thought he was crazy. He certainly *was* a little strange, but Noah was also courageous, a man of great faith and strong will. Against the backdrop of unrelenting ridicule, Noah built a huge ark in the middle of the desert because God told him it was going to rain. No one believed him, but the rains did come and the flood happened, and after the water receded Noah triumphantly left the boat, *got drunk and got naked* (Genesis 9:20–8).

What? *Drunk and naked???* I don't recall any of my Bible teachers or pastors talking about Noah's . . . uh . . .

moment of indiscretion . . . er . . . weakness . . . um . . . failure. The Noah I've always heard about was fiercely faithful, courageously independent and relentlessly resolute. Noah was the model of great faith. Very few ever refer to Noah's losing battle with wine. Maybe being strong and faithful has its down side. Maybe, for flood survivors, life is more complicated than we would like to think, and maybe even Noah could have bouts of depression and loneliness.

Why should I be surprised? Turns out *all* of the biblical characters were a complex mix of strengths and weaknesses. David, Abraham, Lot, Saul, Solomon, Rahab and Sarah were God-loving, courageous, brilliant, fearless, loyal, passionate, committed holy men and women who were also murderers, adulterers and manic depressives. They were men and women who could be gentle, holy defenders of the faith one minute, and insecure, mentally unstable, unbelieving, shrewd, lying, grudge-holding tyrants the next.

The New Testament characters weren't much better. Look who Jesus hung out with. Prostitutes, tax-collectors, adulterers, mental cases, penniless riffraff and losers of all kinds. His own disciples were hardly models of saintliness. The disciples were committed to Jesus, were ready to follow him anywhere (with one notable exception), but they were also troubled by personal infighting, always jockeying for position, suspicious of each other, accusatory, impulsive, selfish, lazy and disloyal. Most of the time they did not understand what

Jesus was talking about, and when he died they had no clue about what to do next. One very clear example of the messiness of the disciples took place in a tiny village.

The disciples were on their way to Jerusalem hoping to stay in a little Samaritan village for the evening. The Samaritans, however, weren't in a mood to co-operate. Most Jews didn't give Samaritans the time of day, so the Samaritans decided to return the favour by making it clear that Jesus and his disciples weren't welcome in their town. James and John (this would be the *beloved* disciple) were furious, storming up to Jesus with a very self-righteous 'Lord, do you want us to call fire down from heaven to destroy them?' (Luke 9:51–6). Not exactly an example of mature discipleship, but a great example of messy discipleship.

You might say Christianity has a tradition of messy spirituality. Messy prophets, messy kings, messy disciples, messy apostles. From God's people going from one mess to another in the Old Testament to most of the New Testament being written to straighten out messes in the Church, the Bible presents a glorious story of a very messy faith.

Sounds like you and I are in good company.

Messy Spirituality unveils the myth of flawlessness and calls Christians everywhere to come out of hiding and stop pretending.

Messy Spirituality has the audacity to suggest that messiness is the workshop of faith, the greenhouse of authentic spirituality – the place the real Jesus meets the real us.

Notorious sinners

A few years ago, I was introduced to a group of uncouth Christians who call themselves 'The Notorious Sinners'. These are men from all walks of life who meet once a year to openly share their messy spirituality with each other. The title 'Notorious Sinners' refers to the scandalous category of forgiven sinners whose reputations and ongoing flaws don't seem to keep Jesus away. In fact, Jesus had a habit of collecting 'disreputables': he called them disciples. He still does. I like people who openly admit their notorious-ness – people who unabashedly confess they are hopelessly flawed and hopelessly forgiven. Graciously, these men invited me to be a part of their group.

The Notorious Sinners meet yearly at spiritual retreat centres where, from the moment we arrive, we find ourselves in trouble with the centre's leadership. We don't act like the majority of contemplatives who come to spiritual retreat centres – reserved, quiet, silently seeking the voice of God. We're a different kind of contemplatives – earthy, boisterous, noisy and rowdy – trampling around our souls seeking God, hanging out with a rambunctious Jesus who is looking for a good time in our hearts. A number of us smoke cigars, about half are recovering alcoholics, and a couple of the men can embarrass a sailor with their language. Two of the Notorious Sinners show up on their Harleys, complete with full leathers.

I admit I run with a rough crowd – Christians whose discipleship is blatantly real and carelessly passionate, characterised by a brazen godliness. Unafraid to admit their flaws, un-intimidated by Christians who deny their messiness, these guys sometimes look like pagans and other times look like Jesus. They are spiritual troublemakers, really, which is why they look like Jesus (who was always causing trouble himself). They are full of mischief, laughter and boisterous behaviour, which is why they look like pagans. Truly messy disciples. The Notorious Sinners are definitely a bizarre mix of the good, the bad and the ugly, living a spirituality which defies simple definitions. Oh, and one more statement about these men: they are some of the most spiritual men I know.

Messy Spirituality is a description of the Christianity most of us live and that few of us admit. It is an attempt to break through the religious wall of secrecy and legitimise the integrity of a faith which is unfinished, incomplete and inexperienced. *Messy Spirituality* is a celebration of a discipleship which is under construction.

Messy Spirituality is the scandalous assertion that following Christ is anything but tidy and neat, balanced and orderly. Far from it. Spirituality is complex, complicated and perplexing – the disorderly, sloppy, chaotic look of authentic faith in the real world.

Spirituality is anything but a straight line: it is a mixed-up, topsy-turvy, helter-skelter godliness that turns our lives into an upside-down toboggan ride full of unexpected turns, surprise bumps and bone-shattering crashes. In other words, messy spirituality is the delirious consequence of a life ruined by a Jesus who will love us right into his arms.

The scandal of spirituality

Jesus is not repelled by us, no matter how messy we are, regardless of how incomplete we are. When we recognise that Jesus is not discouraged by our humanity, not turned off by our messiness, but simply doggedly pursues us in the face of it all, what else can we do but give in to his outrageous, indiscriminate love?

Anne Lamott, a fellow messy Christian, describes perfectly what happens when Jesus pursues us. In her book *Traveling Mercies* Anne recounts her conversion to Jesus. Things were not going well in her life. Addicted to cocaine and alcohol, involved in an affair that produced a child whom she aborted while helplessly watching her best friend dying of cancer, Anne had been periodically visiting a small church. She would sit in the back, listen to the singing and then leave before the sermon. In the week of her abortion she spiralled downhill. Disgusted with herself, she drowned her sorrows in alcohol and drugs. She had been bleeding for many hours from the abortion and finally fell into bed, shaky and sad, smoked a cigarette and turned off the light.

After a while, as I lay there, I became aware of someone with me, hunkered down in the corner, and I just assumed it was my father, whose presence I had felt over the years when I was frightened and alone. The feeling was so strong that I actually turned on the light for a moment to make sure no one was there – of course, there wasn't. But after a while, in the dark again, I knew beyond any doubt that it was Jesus. I felt him as surely as I feel my dog lying nearby as I write this. And I was appalled . . . I thought about what everyone would think of me if I became a Christian, and it seemed an utterly impossible thing that simply could not be allowed to happen. I turned to the wall and said out loud, 'I would rather die.' I felt him just sitting there on his haunches in the corner of my sleeping loft, watching me with patience and love, and I squinted my eyes shut, but that didn't help because that's not what I was seeing him with. Finally I fell asleep, and in the morning, he was gone. This experience spooked me badly, but I thought it was just an apparition, born of fear and self-loathing and booze and loss of blood. But then everywhere I went, I had the feeling that a little cat was following me, wanting me to reach down and pick it up, wanting me to open the door and let it in. But I knew what would happen: you let a cat in one time, give it a little milk, and then it stays for ever. And one week later, when I went back to church, I was so hung over that I couldn't stand up for the songs, and this time I stayed for the sermon, which I just thought was so ridiculous, like someone trying to convince me of the existence of extraterrestrials, but the last song was so deep and raw and pure that I could not escape. It was as if the people were singing in between the notes, weeping and joyful at the same time, and I felt like their voices or *something* was rocking me in its bosom, holding me like a scared kid, and I opened up to that feeling – and it washed over me. I began to cry and left before the benediction, and I raced home and felt the little cat running along at my heels, and I walked down the dock past dozens of potted flowers, under a sky as blue as one of God's own dreams, and I opened the door to my house boat, and I stood there a minute, and then I hung my head and said . . . 'I quit.' I took a long deep breath and said out loud, 'All right. You can come in.' So this was my beautiful moment of conversion.[4]

Anne Lamott is the most improbable candidate for spirituality I could imagine, until I consider my own candidacy. Anne Lamott seems hopelessly messed up, until I remember the mess of my own life. I recognise 'the little cat running along' at Anne Lamott's heels. He's the same 'cat' who's been hounding this messy follower of Christ all my life. No matter how hard I've tried, I've never been able to shake him off. You won't be able to shake him off, either. So we might as well give up, as Anne Lamott did, and let 'the cat' in. Then we can decide what we're going to do with the not-so-little Jesus who, running wild in our hearts, will wreak havoc in our souls, transforming our messy humanity into a messy spirituality.

Messy Spirituality

The place where our messiness and Jesus meet

When we sin and mess up our lives, we find that God doesn't go off and leave us – he enters into our trouble and saves us.

Eugene Peterson[5]

I myself walked up to the Ragman. I told him my name with shame, for I was a sorry figure next to him. Then I took off all my clothes in that place, and I said to him with a dear yearning in my voice: 'Dress me.'

He dressed me, My Lord, he put new rags on me, and I am a wonder beside him.

Walter Wangerin[6]

Our churches are filled with people who outwardly look contented and at peace but inwardly are crying out for someone to love them . . . just as they are – confused, frustrated, often frightened, guilty, and often unable to

communicate even within their own families. But the
other people in the church look so happy and contented
that one seldom has the courage to admit his own deep
needs before such a self-sufficient group as the average
church meeting appears to be.

Keith Miller[7]

He who thinks that he is finished is finished. How true.
Those who think that they have arrived, have lost their
way. Those who think they have reached their goal, have
missed it. Those who think they are saints, are demons.
Henri Nouwen, The Genesee Diary[8]

One of my favourite *Peanuts* cartoons starts with Lucy at
her 5 cent psychology booth, where Charlie Brown has
stopped for advice about life.

'Life is like a deck chair, Charlie,' she says. 'On the
cruise ship of life, some people place their deck chair at
the rear of the ship so they can see where they've been.
Others place their deck chair at the front of the ship so
they can see where they're going.'

The good 'doctor' looks at her puzzled client and asks,
'Which way is your deck chair facing?' Without
hesitating, Charlie replies glumly, 'Heck, I can't get my
deck chair unfolded.'

Charlie and I are soul mates.

Everywhere I look on the cruise ship of Christianity,
I see crews of instructors, teachers, experts and gurus
eager to explain God's plan for the placement of my
deck chair, but I still can't unfold it. No wonder when I
peruse the titles in a Christian book store I feel like I am
the only dumbo in the kingdom of God, a spiritual

nincompoop lost in a ship full of brilliant biblical thinkers, an ungodly midget in a world of spiritual giants. When I compare my life with the experts I feel sloppy, unkempt and messy in the midst of immaculately dressed saints . . . and *I'm a minister*. Maybe that is why God allowed me pastor a church 'for people who don't like to go to church'. When your 'pastor' was kicked out of two Bible colleges, maybe it's easier for people not to be intimidated by some ideal of spirituality.

Many of those who attend our church have always wanted to go to church, wanted to know God better, longed for a better relationship with Jesus, but more often than not would end up at a church where they were made to feel as if the 'mess' of their lives disqualified them from the possibility of an authentic spiritual life. Let me describe for you the 'messy' lives of those who might be sitting in our church on any given Sunday.

Rene

After thirty years of marriage, her husband left her for a younger woman, right after Rene was diagnosed with lung cancer. Devastated and alone, she is slowly trying to follow Jesus in the wreckage of her situation. She was made to feel guilty by her former church because her marriage fell apart, her faith didn't heal the cancer, her children are not in a good place and she is having bouts of depression (which 'spiritual' Christians shouldn't have according to her 'spiritual' friends), wondering what happened to the good life God was supposed to provide for her.

Darrell

Struggling with a long history of abuse and drugs, he usually finds his way to church after a long night of drinking. Darrell sits in the last row, in a seat close to the door, because he doesn't want people to see his swollen face, his too red eyes, his stubble of unshaven beard. He's embarrassed and ashamed that he cannot seem to tame his drinking problem. Again, he has been told at other churches that if he were totally committed to living a spiritual life, drinking wouldn't be a problem. Trying doesn't count, his church friends said to him.

Carol

Divorced, alone. She went through hell last year, dealing with a dying father who required too much of her time because other members of the family refused to do their part. Now she is left with the aftermath of guilt and anger and the struggle with what spirituality looks like in the midst of her ragged and weary day-to-day life. She was told by many of her friends in her previous church that spiritual people don't get divorces, get angry, feel guilty or bear resentment towards their families.

Gary and Linda, Carl and Doreen

Two of many couples who are facing mid-life crisis, empty nest syndromes and haunting questions of 'is this all there is?' These couples are besieged with doubts about Christianity. (Again, in their previous church experiences they were reminded repeatedly that spiritual people don't have mid-life crises, nor are they haunted by doubts and fears because Jesus is the answer to all of their questions and insecurities.)

Lillian, Regina, Don and Barbara
Older members of our church whose spouses have died. They have decided they are too old to start a new relationship. They feel patronised but not befriended, and wonder if their last years will be lived out alone.

The list could go on and on. Sprinkled throughout our congregation are good people who have been paralysed by feelings of inadequacy and unworthiness, insecurity and self-doubt, insignificance and guilt, which is what cripples most of us who are trying to follow Christ.

What does messy spirituality look like?

This may sound shocking to some, but spirituality is a home for those who don't have life figured out, who don't know the Bible as well as they could, and who don't have their spiritual lives all together . . . *the rest of us*, who thought there wasn't a 'rest of us', Christians who are trying *to follow Jesus the best we can*.

A couple of years ago my wife and I sat across the table from a woman we highly respected, a deeply spiritual lady who had profoundly impacted our lives. This woman spent most of her life resisting the noise and activity of the world to seek God in silence and solitude. She had spent literally hundreds of weeks in silent retreat. This was a woman saturated with her faith. You could almost smell God when she came into the room.

We were talking about prayer. 'It's embarrassing to be sitting with you,' I blurted. 'You spend days, weeks, even months in prayer. I'm lucky if I spend ten minutes in prayer. Compared to you, I'm not very spiritual, I'm afraid.'

Her eyes caught mine, flashing with anger, and she fired back, 'Oh, Mike, knock it off. First of all, you don't spend every day with me. You don't know me at all. You are comparing what you know about yourself to what you don't know about me. Secondly, I battle depression daily and it has won during several periods of my life. I never told you about it. I don't have a family, I like to be alone and silent. Trust me, I am just as "un" spiritual as you are.'

Then she said gently, '*You think about God all the time, right?*'

'Well, sort of,' I said.

'Thinking about God is being with God. Being with God is spirituality. Thinking about God is praying. So shut up with this guilt stuff; you have been praying most of your life! You are a spiritual person!'

What?? I've been praying most of my life? What was she talking about? How could anyone accuse *me* of praying all the time when I didn't pray all the time? How could anyone accuse me of being spiritual when I wasn't spiritual? I had no idea spirituality came in unlimited shapes and sizes.

Spirituality looks like whatever you and I look like when we're thinking about Jesus, when we are trying to find Jesus, when we are trying to figure out what real Christianity looks like in the real world. There is no room for pretending in the spiritual life.

Unpretending

Unfortunately, in many religious circles there exists an unwritten rule of the spiritual life. Pretend. Act like God is in control when you don't believe he is. Give the impression everything is okay in your life when it's not. Pretend you believe when you doubt, hide your imperfections, maintain the image of a perfect marriage with healthy and well-adjusted children when your family is like any other normal dysfunctional family. And, whatever you do, don't admit that you sin.

Practically, pretending is efficient, uncomplicated and quick. Answering 'fine' to the question 'How are you doing?' is much easier and quicker than saying, 'Not very well, thank you, my back is bothering me, my teenage children are disappointing me, I'm unhappy with my body, my husband never speaks to me and I'm wondering if Christianity is true.' Honesty requires a huge involvement of time and energy from the person asking the question (who will then wish they'd never asked).

Pretending is the grease of modern non-relationships,

the oil that allows us to perpetuate the illusion of relationships. Pretending allows us to have relationships without having them. Telling the truth, being real, is a synonym for messy spirituality.

Using words like 'messy spirituality' is considered by some people to be rude and audacious. How dare you suggest that people are messy? What are you proposing? Are you suggesting that sin is okay, that we should condone a less than 100 per cent effort to serve God? You are too negative. It's not helpful to emphasise our flaws.

The truth is, we are a mess. None of us is who we appear to be. We all have secrets. We all have issues. We all struggle from time to time. No one is perfect. Not one. (I have just paraphrased Romans 3.) The essence of messy spirituality is the refusal to pretend, to lie or to allow others to believe we are something we are not. Unfortunately, people can handle every issue more easily than they can handle the lack of pretending.

When you and I stop pretending, we expose the pretending of everyone else. The bubble of the perfect Christian life is burst and we all must face the reality of our brokenness.

When my eighteen-month-old daughter was diagnosed with cancer, I was unprepared for the pretending of my Christian friends. Within hours of the news getting out, I was inundated with statements like 'I'm sure God is doing this for a reason', 'God can heal your daughter if you just have faith', 'Even if she dies, she will be better off.' I remember answering these people, 'I hope God is *not* doing this. I don't believe God promises to heal my daughter. Certainly dying is never better than living, otherwise we should all commit suicide.' You can imagine the responses of those around me. They wrote off my statements to shock, bitterness, cynicism and lack of faith. I *wasn't* bitter, I *wasn't* cynical, *I was telling the truth. I could not, would not* pretend any more.

Was I confused about exactly where God was? Of course. Did I have serious questions about my faith? Yes. Was I desperate, depressed, angry, resentful? Yes, I was all those things. I only wish others could have given me the space to be honest, and that they could have been honest too. I look back now, twenty-nine years later, and I realise these people were confused and afraid themselves. If they could get me to agree with them, then they would no longer be afraid. But I couldn't do it. They were forced to deal with the reality of an eighteen-month-old baby who could have died from a terrible disease. (She is very much alive, by the way.) Even today, if you were to ask me why my daughter lived, I would only have one answer: 'I don't know.' I watched a lot of children Lisa's age die during the same period that she was ill, and for the life of me I don't know where God was. I cannot pretend the mystery of God away.

Ministers' sermons are not always amazing masterpieces of truth, wit and insight. Sometimes the sermon just doesn't work, doesn't connect. It simply lies there in a pile while the minister desperately tries to resuscitate it. I was having one of those Sundays. My sermon was just not connecting. People were bored, looking at their watches, and at one point, almost in unison, a majority of the congregation looked back at the clock on the wall. I had no choice, I had to admit the truth. 'I . . . uh . . . realise I've gone on a little long today. Sorry, but I have just one more point I'd like to make.' Sadie, lovely honest Sadie, threw both of her hands to her face and yelled, 'OOOOOH NOOOOO!' causing the rest of the congregation to laugh . . . and then applaud. Most of the people were trying to stifle what they were really feeling, but not Sadie. Luckily her condition of Down's Syndrome doesn't allow her to understand pretending, so she said not only what she thought but what everyone else thought as well.

The sermon was over. Thank God . . . and thank Sadie.

Spiritual people tell the truth. They admit their unfinishedness.

Unfinishedness

Unfinished means incomplete, imperfect, in process, in progress, under construction. Spirituality describes someone who is incomplete, imperfectly living their life for God. The construction site of our soul exposes our flaws, the rough-hewn, not-finished faith clearly visible in our hearts. When we seek God, Jesus begins to take shape in our lives. He *begins* a good work in us, he *starts* changing us, but the finishing process is a more-than-a-lifetime process. The work of God in our lives *will never be finished* until we meet the Finisher. The author of Hebrews said, 'Let us fix our eyes on Jesus, the author and perfecter (*or finisher*) of our faith' (Hebrews 12:2). Spirituality isn't about finishing God's work in us, it's about keeping our eyes on Jesus, the Finisher, who accepts us in our unfinished state.

I'll never forget the day Eric, a recovering alcoholic, stood up in our church during announcements. Eric's lifelong battle with alcohol had been mostly unsuccessful. He was in and out of jail, and his drinking was beginning to take its toll on his marriage. 'I need prayer,' he said. 'My wife has given me an ultimatum – drinking or her. She's asked me to decide today, and I just wanted to tell you all that I have decided . . .' A long awkward pause ensued, and every person in the church was on the edge of their seats, with their faces turned towards him, encouraging him, pleading with him to make the right decision. You could have heard a pin drop. Finally, he stumbled on, tears in his eyes. 'I've decided to choose my wife!' Applause and cheering broke out spontaneously. No one said it, but you could hear it anyway, 'Good answer! Good answer!'

Eric was not afraid to tell the truth, he was not afraid to reveal to all of us how difficult it was to give up alcohol . . . even for his wife. Eric is a spiritual man. Troubled? Yes. Weak? Yes. Unfinished? Absolutely! But Eric told the truth and admitted his desire for drinking was conflicting with his desire to stay married. Eric refused to pretend life was clean and neat, and he knew he had to tell us the way things are, not the way we wish they were.

Jesus understood unfinishedness very well, which is why he was comfortable leaving eleven unfinished disciples. When he died, the disciples were confused, depressed, afraid and doubtful. They faced a lifetime of finishing . . . just like you and me. Messy spirituality not only reminds us we will always be a work in progress, it also reminds us that the unfinished life is a lot more spiritual than we imagined.

Incompetence

Messy spirituality describes our godly incompetence. No one does holy living very well. Spirituality is the humiliating recognition that I don't know how to pray well. I don't understand or know how to navigate God's word properly, and I don't know how to competently live out my commitment to Christ. Messy spirituality affirms our spiritual clumsiness.

I grew up in a church where dancing was frowned upon. As a result, four decades later I still can't dance. Even worship dancing causes my heart to race because I am desperately afraid of anyone seeing the stiff, awkward attempts to make my body move. Because I am a lousy dancer, I avoid any experience where dancing is a possibility.

When it comes to the spiritual life, I am amazed how many of us don't know how to dance. We stand before

God, the music starts playing, and we are embarrassed by our incompetence. The Church has communicated that competence is one of the fruits of the Spirit, and therefore spiritual people are supposed to live faith competently.

One Sunday morning, Gary, a new Christian in our church, offered to read the Scripture for the day, which was the second chapter of Acts. During the worship service I could see Gary in the front row, Bible in hand, checking the service sheet to make sure he wouldn't miss his moment. When the time came, Gary stood up in front of the congregation and began to thumb through his Bible, searching for the book of Acts . . . and searching . . . and searching. Finally, after two awkward minutes, he turned around and said sheepishly, 'Uh, I can find the first book of Acts, but where is the second book of Acts?' Everyone laughed and someone graciously led him to the second *chapter* of the only book of Acts in the Bible. Luckily, our church is a church which expects incompetence. It is amazing to me how many people are afraid of embracing the spiritual life because of the possibility they might say or do the incompetent thing.

Jesus responds to desire. Which is why he responded to people who interrupted him, yelled at him, touched him, screamed obscenities at him, barged in on him, crashed through ceilings to get to him. *Jesus cares more about desire than competence.*

My hunch is that most of you reading this book feel incompetent *and* you can't let go of Jesus. Jesus sees right through your incompetence into a heart longing for him.

It was time for the Scripture reading, and a young girl shuffled towards the front of the church. What a moment for Connie. She had finally mustered up enough courage to ask the pastor if she could read the Scripture. Without hesitation he said yes. For years Connie had stifled her desire to serve in the church because of her 'incompetencies'. Reading was extremely difficult for her, and Connie had a terrible time enunciating clearly. But she had been in this church many years, and she was beginning to understand the grace of God. Jesus didn't just die for our sins, he died so people who couldn't read or speak could read and speak. Now she could serve the Jesus she loved so much. Now she could express her desire for God in a tangible, visible way.

The time for the Scripture reading had arrived. Connie kept walking. Her steps were laboured: she had one leg shorter than the other, causing her body to teeter from side to side. Finally Connie was standing at the front, looking at the congregation with pride and joy. The congregation was silent. Too silent.

Silence can sometimes be excruciatingly loud. The screaming silence was covering up the congregation's discomfort. Clearly, most of them were trying to understand what Connie was doing at the front and they were trying not to notice her many incompetencies. Her eyes were too close together and her head twisted back and forth at odd angles while her face wrenched from one distorted grimace to another.

The reading began. Stammering, stuttering, Connie stumbled proudly through the passage in a long continuum of untranslatable sounds, garbled sentences, long torturous pauses and jumbled phrases. Finally, the reading was over and the congregation was exhausted.

Connie didn't notice the exhaustion. She was ecstatic. Her face seemed no longer distorted, only full of joy. Her cheeks were flushed with pride, her eyes sparkling with the joy of accomplishment, her heart warm with knowing she had *served* the congregation, participated in her faith. Yes, she would remember this day for a long time. How wonderful it was, she thought, to no longer be a *spectator* in church – she *was* the church this morning!

Thank God her mental capacities were limited. Thank God she was not able to discern the faces of the congregation, or she would have crumbled in despair. Thank God she wasn't able to sense what people were really thinking.

Because almost everyone in the congregation was thinking, 'THIS WAS AN OUTRAGE!' I know this is what they were thinking because the senior pastor, my father, was ordered to attend an emergency church council meeting after the service.

'How did this happen?' they demanded. '*What* were you thinking?'

'Connie wanted to read the Scripture,' he replied softly.

'Well, let her stand at the door and hand out books, or help with the post, but don't let her read! The girl can't read or speak, for God's sake! Her reading took *ten minutes*!'

'The church,' they said, *'is not a place for incompetence.'*

My father believes, as I do, that the church is the place where the incompetent, the unfinished and even the unhealthy are welcome. I believe Jesus agrees.

Desperateness

Christianity is not for people who think religion is a pleasant distraction, a nice alternative or a positive influence. Messy spirituality is the term we use to describe the place where desperation meets Jesus. More often than not, in Jesus' day, desperate people who tried to get to Jesus were surrounded by religious people who either ignored or rejected the ones seeking to have their hunger for God filled. Sadly, not much has changed over the years.

Desperate people don't do well in churches. They don't fit and they don't co-operate in the furthering of their starvation. 'Church' people often label 'desperate' people as strange, odd and unbalanced. But when desperate people get a taste of God, they can't stay away from him, no matter what everyone around them thinks.

'Desperate' is a strong word. That is why I like it. People who are desperate are rude, frantic and reckless. Desperate people are explosive, focused, uncompromising in their desire to get what they want. When someone is desperate they will crash through the veil of niceness in order to get what they want. (The New Testament is filled with desperate people, people who barged into private dinners, screamed at Jesus until they had his attention or destroyed the roof of someone's house to get to him.) People who are desperate for spirituality very seldom worry about the mess they make on their way to be with Jesus.

Barbara Brown Taylor pastored an inner-city church for many years. The sanctuary was open during the day, but unfortunately, because of the kind of world we live in, a closed circuit camera was installed to monitor what went on inside. The receptionist of the church checked the monitor throughout the day. One day, during a staff meeting, the receptionist interrupted the meeting to report, 'There's a man lying face down on the altar steps. I wouldn't bother you, but he's been there for hours. Every now and then he stands up, raises his arms towards the altar, and lies down again.' One of the staff went out to speak to the man and find out if he was okay, and then reported back, 'He says he's praying.' They decided to leave the man alone. But he returned every day, lying on the altar steps. His clothes were worn and dirty; his hair was in knots. The staff instructed the sexton and the altar guild not to disturb the man and to work around him. Finally it was Sunday, and as Barbara entered the sanctuary for the early service she saw the man again, blocking her path to the altar. She was afraid. What if he was crazy? She approached him cautiously, noticing how dirty he was, how emaciated he was from lack of food. She explained to him that a service was to begin in a few minutes and that he would have to leave. He lifted

his forehead from the floor and, speaking with a heavy
Haitian accent, he said, 'That's okay.' Barbara then
described what happened after he left.

> The eight o'clock service began on time. The faithful
> took their places and I took mine. We read our parts
> well. We spoke when we were supposed to speak and
> were silent when we were supposed to be silent. We
> offered up our symbolic gifts, we performed our
> bounden duty and service, and there was nothing
> wrong with what we did, nothing at all. We were good
> servants, careful and contrite sinners who had come
> for our ritual cleansing, but one of us was missing. He
> had risen and gone his way, but the place where he lay
> on his face for hours – making a spectacle of himself
> – seemed all at once so full of heat and light that I
> stepped around it on my way out, chastened if only
> for that moment by the call to a love so excessive, so
> disturbing, so beyond the call to obedience that it
> made me want to leave all my good works behind.[9]

(I wish the man had been invited to stay for the worship
service. Maybe Barbara did invite him and he declined.
Whatever, I believe Jesus would have asked him to stay.)
A desperate man, covered with dirt and with hair clotted
from days of abuse, filled a sanctuary with the spectacle
of God's presence.

When the unqualified are qualified

Walking by a pet shop on his way to school, a young boy stopped and stared into the window. Inside were four black puppies, playing together. After school he ran home, pleading with his mother to let him have one of the puppies. 'I'll take care of it, Mum, I will. If you can just give me an advance on my pocket money, I'll have enough money to buy one with my own money. Please, Mum, please.' The mother, knowing full well the complications of a new puppy in a busy household, just couldn't resist her son.

'Okay, you can get the puppy, but I will expect you to take care of it.'

'Yes, Mum, I will.'

Filled with excitement, the little boy ran to the pet shop to buy his new puppy. After determining he had enough money, the pet shop owner brought the boy over to the window to choose his puppy. After a few minutes the young boy said, 'Um . . . I'll take the little one in the corner.'

'Oh no,' said the shop owner, 'not that one, he's crippled. Notice how he just sits there? Something is wrong with one of his legs so he can't run and play like the rest of the puppies. Chose another one.'

Without saying a word, the boy reached down and lifted his trouser-leg to expose a chrome leg brace to the owner, 'No,' he said firmly, 'I think I'll take the puppy in the corner.'[10]

It turned out that what disqualified the puppy from being chosen by others most qualified him to be chosen by the little boy. It turns out what disqualifies you and me from spirituality – the mess of our lives and our crippled-ness – most qualifies us to be chosen by Jesus. It is amazing how few of us believe in the unqualified grace of God. Oh, yes, God loves us, as long as we're clean and whole and fixed.

The myth of fixing ourselves

For a period of time we were lucky enough to have a cleaner. She would come in once a week to dust, vacuum and clean every little out-of-the-way corner of our house. I dreaded the day the cleaner came, because my wife and I would spend all morning *cleaning the house for the cleaner!* We didn't want the house to be dirty, or what would the cleaner think!

We act the same way with God. We talk our way out of the spiritual life by refusing to come to God as we are. Instead, we decide to wait until we are ready to come to God as we aren't. We decide that the way we lived yesterday, last week or last year makes us 'damaged' goods, and that until we start living 'right' we're not 'God material'. Some of us actually believe that until we choose the correct way to live, we aren't choose-able; until we clean up the mess, Jesus won't have anything to do with us. The opposite is true. *Until we admit we are a mess* Jesus won't have anything to do with us. Once we admit how unlovely we are, how unattractive we are, how lost we are, Jesus shows up unexpectedly.

According to the New Testament, Jesus is attracted to the unattractive. He prefers the lost ones over the 'found ones', the losers over the winners, the broken instead of the whole, the messy instead of the unmessy, the crippled instead of the non-crippled.

Dancing the undance-able

Lost in my thoughts, I was sitting in a hotel ballroom with fifteen hundred college students participating in a college weekend faith conference. On the last day of the conference, with classes starting the following Monday, the students made it clear they wanted to prolong the conference as long as possible. They wanted to party, to dance the afternoon away, to celebrate the Lord of the dance – to resist going back into the busyness and demands of college life. The morning general session turned into a spontaneous celebration. Young men and women raised their hands, stood on chairs, shouted, cried and laughed, and suddenly a conga line broke out. Within seconds hundreds of students were weaving in and out of the room in long, raucous lines, praising their God.

An older man with cerebral palsy sat in a motorised wheelchair, watching while everyone else partied. (He wasn't a student. Technically he wasn't even supposed to be at the conference.) I was seated next to him, watching the students celebrate, when suddenly the wheelchair lunged forward into the celebration. The man's arms were waving, his chair was careening around the room with a jerky, captivating motion, his mouth was struggling to open and shut, making incomprehensible sounds. Somehow a man who couldn't dance had become part of the graceful dancing of the crowd. Without warning, the man's motorised wheelchair lurched forward to the base of the stage, racing back and forth through a series of figure eights, twirls and circles. He was laughing, lost in the joy of the Lord. His joy had taken a cold, ugly piece of motorised machinery and transformed it into an extension of his unconfined worship. He and his wheelchair had become one, a dancing, living thing. This man with a crippled body found a way to break free from the rigid, cold, restrictive wheelchair, and was dancing the undance-able.

I envy the man in the wheelchair. I want my crippled soul to escape the cold and sterile spirituality of a religion where only the perfect, non-disabled get in. I want to lurch forward to Jesus, where the unwelcome receive welcome and the unqualified get qualified. I want to hear Jesus tell me I can dance when everyone else says that I can't. I want to hear Jesus walk over to me and whisper to this handicapped, messy Christian, 'Do you want to dance?'

Resisting the Resisters

Overcoming the saboteurs of spirituality

Our deepest fear is not that we are inadequate. Our deepest fear is that we are powerful beyond measure. It is our light, not our darkness, that most frightens us. We ask ourselves, Who am I to be brilliant, gorgeous, talented, and fabulous? Actually, who are you not to be? You are a child of God. Your playing small doesn't serve the world. There is nothing enlightened about shrinking so that other people won't feel insecure around you.

Nelson Mandela[11]

Miracles Happen
Somebody loves me
I am not alone
The majority isn't always right
Wonderful things happen in dungeons
Death is only skin deep
Poverty is temporary and so is wealth

He who dies with the most toys loses the most toys
You can always go home again
Things may look a lot better in three days.
                                    Donna Maclean[12]

They were good in the worst sense of the word.
                          Mark Twain (source unknown)

No punishment anyone might inflict on them could
possibly be worse that the punishment they inflict on
themselves by conspiring in their own diminishment.
                                    Parker Palmer[13]

A blind man sits by the roadside begging. Suddenly a huge crowd moves down the road, jostling past him. He asks some questions and realises Jesus is passing by.

His heart begins to race, 'Jesus of Nazareth! This is the one they say can heal blindness! This is my chance to be freed from blindness. All my life I have wanted to see and my chance is now.' He gets to his feet and begins to yell, 'JESUS, SON OF DAVID, HAVE MERCY ON ME!' (Luke 18:35–42).

Instantly the crowd shouts back to the blind man, 'Shut up! Keep quiet!' Everyone around the blind man tries to silence him, to keep him from creating a scene, to keep him from 'annoying' Jesus.

It is the nature of human beings, the nature of modern life, to silence those who interrupt our routine activity and our routine understandings. We don't like those who speak up, who leave the status quo, who refuse to keep quiet, who reject compliance as a way of life. And when it comes to faith, people would much rather we shut up than say disturbing things about what genuine faith looks like.

The silencers

Religious institutions do not like surprises, and they especially dislike a spirituality which threatens the status quo. Threaten others with a loud and boisterous faith, and you will be politely (at first) asked to quieten down; dance your faith instead of sitting still in your pew, and you will be asked to leave; talk about your faith with passion, and expect expressions of concern about the inappropriateness of your emotions. Allow others to see your brokenness, and find yourself reprimanded for being too open; hear the music of faith, and watch others warn you of the danger of emotional instability.

Shel Silverstein has written a wonderful poem about those who have been silenced:

> You should have heard the old men cry,
> You should have heard the biddies
> When that sad stranger raised his flute
> And piped away the kiddies.
> Katy, Tommy, Meg and Bob
> Followed, skipping gaily,
> Red-haired Ruth, my brother Rob,
> And little crippled Bailey,
> John and Mils and Cousin Claire,
> Dancin', spinnin', turnin'

'Cross the hills to God knows where –
They never came returnin'.
'Cross the hills to God knows where
The piper pranced, a-leadin'
Each child in Hamlin Town but me,
And I stayed home unheedin'.
My papa says that I was blest
For if that music found me,
I'd be witch-cast like all the rest.
This town grows old around me.
I cannot say I did not hear
That sound so haunting hollow –
I heard, I heard, I heard it clear . . .
I was afraid to follow.[14]

Pity the one who stayed. Cry a tear for the one who heard and was afraid to follow. Mourn for the one who didn't heed, the one who let the town grow old around him. Pity all of us who are surrounded by those who are afraid to follow the 'sad stranger', the one who came to get us all 'dancin', spinnin' and turnin''

But those of us who have heard the haunting sound of Jesus' voice, those of us who sense life and hope and adventure in the gospel, those of us who are willing to speak up, to question the deadness around us, to express our desire for life – we must not keep quiet even if everyone around us tells us we are crazy.

And the crowd will call you crazy.

And the masses will try to silence you.

I was speaking at a conference recently and I mentioned that a woman in my church – whom I deeply respect and who is one of the most godly women I know – smokes and sometimes uses colourful language. After the talk, I was made aware of a pastor in the audience who was outraged by what I'd said. He was so angry he demanded that everyone from his church no longer listen to my talks. After the conference, trying to understand what he was so upset about, I contacted him. 'How dare you tell the audience that "one of the most godly women you know" smokes and uses the language of the world?' he said, quite heatedly.

'Because she *is* one of the most godly women I know, and she *does* happen to smoke and use "colourful" language,' I replied.

The conversation went on for a long time, and he was not impressed with my defence of this woman. Although he didn't use these words, what he was saying was clear: 'Godly women do not smoke, nor do they use 'colorful' language! Full stop.' In his spiritual world, there is no place for smoking, swearing, godly women. He didn't want to hear otherwise. No exceptions.

In the real world where I live, this woman is not an exception and remains one of the most godly women I know.

The assault of the comfortable

There is a tendency in all of us to seek comfort, to structure predictability, to eliminate 'new and different' from our experience. The word 'messy' strikes fear into the hearts of the comfortable. According to the comfortable, God does what he always does. 'God is the same yesterday, today and tomorrow' they interpret as '*God stays the same*'. There are those in the Church who honestly believe God is a nice and neat God. One quick run through the Bible gives you a different picture. The God of the Bible is the master of surprises: frightening clouds of smoke and fire, earthquakes, windstorms and firestorms, donkeys that talk, pillars of salt, oceans splitting apart, using a little boy to kill Goliath, Messiah in swaddling clothes and dying on a cross. No one can follow God and be comfortable for long.

An attractive young woman, on the fast track towards a lucrative business career, decided she wanted to delay her career plans to work with inner-city young people. God had been working in her heart and she felt a real sense of calling. She was hired by a church where the ethnic mix was changing, and within weeks she was working with gang members. She successfully persuaded a few gang members to attend a Bible study at the church. One night she was talking about Matthew 6:33 ('But seek first his kingdom and his righteousness . . .'), explaining that if you want to be a disciple of Jesus nothing can be more important than him. Her words were: 'If the gang is more important than Jesus, then the gang has to go. If your girlfriend is more important than Jesus, then the girlfriend has to go.' One of the gang members was so into what she was saying that, after those words, he reacted violently by throwing his arms back, yelling, 'Dude, it's hard to be a disciple!' and his elbow crashed through a window. When the church found out, they were very upset at having to pay out to fix the window and banned the gang members from using the room.

Here was a young woman teaching gang members about Jesus, and they were listening. She was doing such a good job that her students understood how costly faith is. What a teacher! But all the *church* could think about was broken windows.

But it gets worse.

A few weeks later, the pastor accidentally interrupted one of the gang Bible studies. He sat down and spent a few minutes talking with the gang members. After he left, one of the lads said, 'Hey, I like that guy. Let's go to church this Sunday.' The youth worker decided to seat the gang members in the balcony rather than with the congregation downstairs. When the minister came out and announced the giving of the peace, one of the gang members spontaneously stood up and yelled, 'Hey, dude, you are cool!' The congregation turned around in shock. After the service, the youth worker was told not to bring the gang members back to the church until they had learned how to behave *inside* a church.

The church should have turned around and invited the gang members downstairs. They should have applauded a woman who was doing an amazing job of evangelism. Instead, the youth worker was fired. Apparently this church was more concerned about comfort than it was about a group of gang members' discomforting search for spirituality.

Seek the spiritual life, admit your messiness, follow Christ wherever he leads you, and discomfort is right round the corner.

A group of us in ministry have been acquainted for years. We meet together two or three times a year and share life stories, pray and worship together. True, we are not the closest of friends, but we know each other very well. Or so we thought. A few months ago we were sitting around the table catching up on the conditions of our lives and one person put a cassette recorder on the table, announcing he wanted to play a tape for us. It was a recording of a recent testimony he had given at his church. I cannot describe for you the shock on all of our faces as our friend's voice on tape told of a lifelong struggle with alcohol, which he had managed to hide from his wife, from his children and from all of us. I must admit, it took a lot of courage for our friend to share the pain of the years of hiding his addiction.

When the tape finished, the silence lasted a long time. Each of us was confronting our own secrets which were still secret. Each of us was struggling with the shock and resulting discomfort of realising we didn't know our friend very well. In fact, we were reluctantly realising, we didn't know anyone in our group very well. You could cut the awkwardness with a knife. Of course, our friend sat there petrified that his openness would cause us to reject him, to be angry because he hadn't said anything before now – or worse, that we would judge him as unfit to call himself a Christian and label him as a phoney, or untrustworthy.

The attack of the name-callers

When Jesus and his followers show up, it doesn't take long before people start pointing fingers and calling names. Jesus was called all kinds of names: 'wine-bibber' (what is a wine-bibber, anyway?), 'Sabbath breaker' and 'blasphemer'. Over the centuries, religious people have refined name-calling to an art. The name most commonly used today? *Unspiritual!*

Because our church is a church for people 'who don't like to go to church', many of our members have been called names by a church (which is why they don't like to go to church) or by those who attend a church.

The body of Christ can be mean.

If a person is trying to follow Christ and others are concerned about what they are doing or how they are doing it, name-calling can become vicious.

Her name was Margaret. For almost forty years she had lived with the memory of one soul-scarring day in a one-roomed school with twenty-five students aged from six to fourteen. From the very first day, Margaret and her bitter and harsh teacher, Miss Garner, didn't get along. Over the years, the animosity between them only worsened, until one fateful autumn day, when nine-year-old Margaret's life was for ever altered.

Margaret frantically raced into her classroom after break, late again. Miss Garner was furious. 'Margaret!' she shouted, 'We have been waiting for you! Get up here to the front of the class, right now!' Margaret walked slowly to the teacher's desk and was told to face the class, and then the nightmare began. Miss Garner ranted, 'Boys and girls, Margaret has been a bad girl. I have tried to help her be responsible. But apparently she doesn't want to learn. So we must teach her a lesson. We must force her to face what a selfish person she has become. I want each of you to come to the front of the room, take a piece of chalk and write something bad about Margaret on the blackboard. Maybe this experience will motivate Margaret to become a better person!'

Margaret stood frozen next to Miss Garner. One by one, the pupils began a silent procession to the blackboard. One by one, the pupils wrote their life-smothering words, slowly dousing the light in Margaret's soul, 'Margaret is stupid!' 'Margaret is selfish!' 'Margaret is fat!' 'Margaret is a dummy!' On and on they went, until twenty-five terrible scribblings of Margaret's 'badness' screamed from the blackboard.

Each ugly indictment cut Margaret's heart like a knife. The venomous sentences taunted her in what felt like the longest day of her life. After walking home with each caustic word indelibly written on her soul, she crawled into her bed, claiming sickness, and tried to cry the pain away. But the pain never left, and forty years later she slumped down in the psychologist's waiting room, her life still cringing in the shadow of twenty-five sentences. To her horror, Margaret had slowly become what the students had written.

Margaret's teacher knew exactly what she was doing. She knew the power of name-calling. Margaret was humiliated by the thoughtless and cruel act of a teacher, robbed of the sparkle in her eye, cursed to live the rest of her life in the shadow of a nightmarish experience in the schoolroom.

I believe many of us have experienced the humiliation of Margaret.

One day we decided to become a follower of Christ, to seek his presence in our life, and we were doing our best to keep Jesus in our sights when we were shocked to discover our fellow 'classmates' called us names. 'Ungodly.' 'Uncommitted.' 'Poor example.' 'Unspiritual.' 'Carnal.' 'Unbiblical.' In other words, 'You are "doing God" all wrong.'

The who-so-evers and just-anyones

According to his critics, *Jesus* 'did God' all wrong. He went to the wrong places, said the wrong things and, worst of all, he let just anyone into the kingdom. Jesus scandalised the arrogance of an intimidating, elitist, country-club religion by opening membership in the spiritual life to those who had been denied membership. What made people furious was Jesus' irresponsible habit of throwing open the doors of his love to the who-so-evers, the just-anyones and not-a-chancers like you and me.

Nothing makes people in the Church more angry than grace. A strange phenomenon occurs: we stumble into a party we weren't invited to, and then we find the uninvited standing at the door making sure no other uninviteds gets in. Once we are included in the party because of Jesus' 'irresponsible' love, we decide to make grace 'more responsible', becoming self-appointed Kingdom Monitors, guarding the kingdom of God, keeping the riffraff out (which, as I understand it, is who the kingdom of God is supposed to include).

John tells the story of a man like us – an outsider, a blind outsider. The blind man bumped into Jesus, found his blindness 'ruined' by Jesus and became a scandal to the religious leaders of his day. His miraculous encounter with Jesus is a model for all of us who are trying to live spiritual lives. In chapter 9 of John's Gospel, we meet a man blind from birth, sitting in his familiar place, begging. The disciples bring up some theological questions about him. They are not concerned about *the blind man*, what they are concerned about is the *theology* of blindness. They are not filled with compassion, they are filled with questions – philosophical questions. The disciples attempt to have a theological discussion and Jesus cuts it short. He makes it very clear that what matters is glorifying God, helping blind men and women see. The disciples are worried about theories and doctrines. *Jesus is worried about the blind man.*

In effect, Jesus is saying, 'Your philosophising about the cause of blindness is interesting, but *wait until you see this!* Talking about God's power is one thing, but look what happens when you are in the presence of his power. A little mud, a little water, and the blind man is no longer blind.'

Now the man's troubles really begin! When blind people get unblind, sometimes their closest friends are not happy. Meeting Jesus does not always result in our troubles ending – sometimes our troubles just begin.

The Condemners

From the beginning of his encounter with Jesus, the blind man is in trouble. Jesus tried to warn us: 'Do not suppose that I have come to bring peace to the earth. I did not come to bring peace, but a sword.' Begin a relationship with Jesus, and we're going to get into the same kind of trouble Jesus did.

When the man who was formerly blind shows up in his neighbourhood, his neighbours refuse to believe he can see. Afraid of mystery, unable to fathom the possibility of a miracle, the neighbours turn their backs on their friend and drag him to those who should have known something about mystery, miracle and spirituality – the religious leaders – the Condemners. The sabotage of the blind man began.

How should you and I respond to intimidation? How can we survive when those around us criticise our spirituality or, worse, reject us because we're not religious enough? The blind man gives us some helpful clues.

Living our 'ignorance'

The Pharisees, the theologians of the day, the Kingdom Monitors, who knew Scripture like the backs of their hands (instead of knowing it in the fronts of their hearts) should have been ready to celebrate. Instead, they were ready to condemn.

'Tell us, Mr Blind Man, how did you get your eyesight back?'

The man's answer is very bizarre. 'A stranger made mud with his own spit, stuck it in my eyes and ordered me to wash the mud off in the pool of Siloam. I did what he said. Now I can see.'

The blind man flunks religion. Nought out of ten.

The Kingdom Monitors know more about God than an uneducated, uncouth blind man, or so they believe. A heated lecture ensues. 'Any Sunday School student knows that people who are blind from birth are paying for the sins of their family. The real God doesn't use mud to heal people, especially from self-appointed "prophets" no one has heard of. And, most certainly, *God doesn't heal on the Sabbath.*'

Religious people love to hide behind religion. They love the rules of religion more than they love Jesus. With practice, Condemners let rules become more important than the spiritual life.

John Mackie was the president of the Church of Scotland after World War II. With two other ministers from a rather severe and pietistic denomination, he travelled to some remote parts of the Balkan peninsula to check on missionaries they supported in rural parts of the country.

The three clergymen called on an Orthodox priest in a small Greek village. Excited to see the visitors, the priest offered the clergymen a glass of rare and expensive wine. Horrified, the two pietistic ministers refused. Dr Mackie, on the other hand, took a glassful, sniffed it like a wine connoisseur, sipped it and praised its quality. He even asked for another glass. His companions were noticeably upset by Dr Mackie's behaviour.

Later, when the three men were in the jeep again and making their way up the rough road out of the village, the two pious clergymen turned on Dr Mackie with a vengeance. 'Dr Mackie,' they insisted, 'do you mean to tell us that you are the president of the Church of Scotland and an officer of the World Council of Churches and you drink?'

Dr Mackie had had all he could take and his Scottish temper got the better of him. 'No, dammit, I don't,' he said, 'but *somebody* had to be a Christian!'[15]

My hunch is that Dr Mackie didn't convince his Condemners. The rules of their faith were much more important than showing grace. They were much more excited about condemning the faith of Dr Mackie and the priest than they were about living their own faith.

The Condemners try to force the blind man to renounce Jesus. They ask him to confirm that Jesus is anything but a Messiah – that in fact he is a sinner.

What can the blind man possibly say to defend himself?

He trusts his ignorance.

'Whether he [Jesus] is a sinner or not, I don't know. One thing I do know, *I was blind but now I see!*' The blind man does the only thing he can: he tells his strange, contradictory, politically incorrect, irrational story. He tells the truth, the sum total of his theological training – which, by the way, is where all good theology starts: it starts with the truth.

Brennan Manning tells the story of a recent convert to Jesus who was approached by an unbelieving friend:

'So you have been converted to Christ?'
'Yes.'
'Then you must know a great deal about him. Tell me, what country was he born in?'
'I don't know.'
'What was his age when he died?'
'I don't know.'

'How many sermons did he preach?'

'I don't know.'

'You certainly know very little for a man who claims to be converted to Christ.'

'You are right. I am ashamed at how little I know about him. But this much I know: three years ago I was a drunkard. I was in debt. My family was falling to pieces; they dreaded the sight of me. But now I have given up drink. We are out of debt. Ours is a happy home. My children eagerly await my return home each evening. All this Christ has done for me. This much I know of Christ![16]

Maybe the alcoholic and the blind man didn't know much about Jesus, but they knew plenty about their *encounters* with Jesus. The alcoholic and the blind man may not have studied biblical history, but their lives had been changed by the Truth . . . and the Pharisees (then and now) knew it.

Armed with their superior education, their flawless theology and the power of their religion, the Pharisees desperately try to regain control by attacking with questions. 'Is Jesus of the devil? Where is he? What do you know about him?'

The blind man knew very little about Jesus, but he was an expert in first-time-seeing. He couldn't explain where Jesus was, but he knew what Jesus did. He couldn't define a Messiah, but he certainly could describe what it was like to see a flower for the first time. When confronted with questions about Jesus, the blind man was not afraid to say, 'I don't know.'

'I don't know' is often the only reply we can give to explain the mystery of Christ.

Jesus often left his followers 'I don't know-ing'. Our personal relationship with Christ is often the only apologetic we can offer. Our lack of knowing is the beginning of humility and the very essence of the spiritual life.

The intimidated becomes the intimidator

Dragged before his neighbours, his family, and the Pharisees . . . the blind man is pummelled by all of them. His neighbours don't believe him, his parents abandon him and the Pharisees attack him physically, as well as emotionally. They try to intimidate him, to shut him up.

But the blind man will not shut up. Apparently, a few minutes *with* Jesus teaches us more about God than a lifetime of studying *about* God. (*Trust your relationship with Jesus!*) And then, without warning, the lectured-*to* becomes the lecture*r*. 'What's the matter with you guys? You don't know who this man is, yet he opened my eyes on command! God doesn't listen to sinners, yet he listened to this man! Hmmm. Makes me think he must be from God, because if he weren't, how could he have done what he just did?'

The Pharisees were so enraged they physically threw the blind man out of the synagogue, leaving him alone.

Telling the truth can get you killed . . . or, at the least, beaten up.

And here is the biggest tragedy of all. Not one person in the entire ninth chapter of John, including the blind man's parents, did what any follower of Christ should have done . . . *throw a party!* When a man or woman has just received their sight after a lifetime of blindness, someone should order the wine, start the music and *begin the celebration!* The spiritual life is not just about rules and regulations, teaching and theology, lectures and sermons. Life with Jesus is meant to be lived – not smothered, dissected, inspected or condemned. The blind man should have had the time of his life! His moment of healing should have been commemorated as a moment he would never forget.

One of my son's friends (I'll call him Greg) recently celebrated his twenty-eighth birthday. Greg's parents were not happy with his life choices, especially his decision to live with his girlfriend. Knowing his parents' displeasure, Greg and his girlfriend decided to get married, and they phoned his parents to give them the good news. 'We want to be married in Minnesota, so the entire family can come.' Greg's parents were happy, but restrained.

While they were planning the wedding, Greg's girlfriend discovered she was pregnant. Realising the coming pregnancy would upset his parents, Greg decided to call off the big family wedding and use the money they were going to spend on the ceremony for their new baby instead.

Greg and Diane opted for a civil wedding with a registrar presiding. Only my son and his girlfriend witnessed the union.

A couple of weeks later, my son and his girlfriend were with some friends and the subject of Greg's marriage came up. Everyone concluded that it was more like a 'non-wedding' – impersonal and isolated. As Greg and Diane's friends talked, their conviction grew. No wedding should be an impersonal, isolated, bureaucratic, legal transaction. Weddings should be celebrated. The couple should be surrounded with the support and care of family and friends. The group looked at each other and almost in unison said the same thing, 'Why don't we give Greg and Diane the wedding they never had?' As soon as the words had left their mouths, they knew what had to be done. Even though Greg and Diane were legally married, the group decided to make them a present of a 'real' wedding. The date was set, both families were contacted, and surprisingly they all agreed to come to the surprise wedding at their own expense. Sixty friends and family were involved in a conspiracy of grace.

To ensure that the couple were available on their new wedding day, Greg and Diane were invited to my son's home for a 'dress-up' dinner on the day of the wedding conspiracy. When they arrived for dinner, a group of Diane and Greg's friends kidnapped each of them separately and took them off to the send-off they'd never had. The 'bride' and 'groom' were separately driven to a secluded place where, seated in a circle with their samegender friends, they were asked a series of questions like, 'Now that you have been married for three months, what mistakes have you made?' and 'How can we help you in your marriage?' Both the young husband and wife were given a picture of their spouse and asked to write on the back of the photo all the reasons they loved that person.

When the individual parties were finished, Greg and Diane thought that the surprise was over. You can imagine their shock when they were returned to the house, only to discover sixty of their family and friends waiting for them, laughing, yelling 'Surprise!!!' The hugging began, and it took Greg and Diane a long time to stop crying. After they regained their composure, the entire group moved into the garden, where a minister was waiting, surrounded with flowers. The couple exchanged vows, each parent vowed their support, and each friend walked by and whispered a blessing to the couple. When the service was completed, there wasn't a dry eye anywhere. Everyone left knowing they had participated in a moment of grace. This wedding had 'Jesus' written all over it.

The Kingdom Protectors would raise their voices immediately. 'You can't do this!!! You are condoning the sins of two young people who lived together and conceived a baby before they were married. Real Christians do not condone unbiblical living!!!' And they would be correct. Christians do not *condone* unbiblical living, we *redeem* it. Greg and Diane were able to glimpse forgiveness and redemption in one grace-filled experience.

Jesus rights the wrongs

At the end of the story are these words, 'Jesus heard that they had thrown him [the blind man] out, and when he had *found* him . . .' Jesus did not forget the blind man. He did not abandon him, but sought him out, came after him and found him – 'wrong' answers, 'wrong' explanations, 'wrong' theology and all. Jesus finds you and me, and says, I think, the same thing He said to a woman who faced the condemnation of everyone around her: 'Has no one condemned you? *Then neither do I condemn you!*'

Remember Margaret, the young girl we met at the beginning of the chapter? After decades of depression and anxiety, Margaret finally sought help. Two long years of weekly counselling helped her to finally extricate herself from her past. It had been a long and difficult road, but today was the last meeting with her psychologist. She smiled at her counsellor (how long it had been since she'd smiled!) as they talked about her readiness to move on.

'Well, Margaret,' the counsellor said softly, 'I guess it's graduation day for you. How are you feeling?'

After a long silence Margaret spoke. 'I . . . I'm okay.'

The counsellor hesitated, 'Margaret, I know this will be difficult, but just to make sure you're ready to move on, I am going to ask you to do something very difficult. I want you to go back to your classroom and detail the events of that day. Take your time. Describe each of the children as they approached the blackboard, remember what they wrote and how you felt – all twenty-five of them.'

In some ways, this would be easy for Margaret. For forty years she had remembered every detail. And yet, to go through the nightmare once more would take every bit of strength she had. After a long silence she began the painful description of that day. One by one, she described each of the pupils vividly, as though she had just seen them, stopping periodically to regain her composure, forcing herself to face each one of those pupils one more time.

Finally she came to the end, and the tears would not stop, could not stop. Margaret cried for a long time before she realised someone was gently whispering her name. 'Margaret. Margaret. Margaret.'

She looked up to see her counsellor staring directly into her eyes, saying her name over and over again. Margaret stopped crying for a moment.

'Margaret. You . . . you left out one person.'

'I certainly did *not*! I have lived with this story for forty years. I know every detail by heart.'

'No, Margaret, you did forget someone. See, he's sitting in the back of the classroom. He's standing up, walking towards your teacher, Miss Garner. She is handing him a piece of chalk and he's taking it, Margaret, he's taking it! Now he's walking over to the blackboard and picking up a rubber. *He is rubbing out every one of the sentences the students wrote.* They are gone! Margaret, they are gone!

Now he's turning and looking at you, Margaret. Do you recognise him yet? Yes, his name is Jesus. Look, he's writing new sentences on the board. "Margaret is loved." "Margaret is beautiful." "Margaret is gentle and kind." "Margaret is strong." "Margaret has great courage."

And Margaret began to weep again. But very quickly the weeping turned into a smile, and then into laughing, and then into tears of joy.[17]

After forty dark years, Margaret was no longer condemned, no longer alone and no longer rejected. The blindness of her past horror was removed. Margaret and a certain blind man . . . and maybe even you and I . . . can shout with confidence, 'Once I was blind, but now I see!!'

The Ugliness of Rejection

Paralysed by our past

How unutterably sweet is the knowledge that our Heavenly Father knows us completely. No talebearer can inform on us, no enemy can make an accusation stick; nor forgotten skeleton can come tumbling out of some hidden closet to abash us and expose our past; no unsuspected weakness in our characters can come to light to turn God away from us, since He knew us utterly before we knew Him and called us to Himself in the full knowledge of everything that was against us.

A. W. Tozer[18]

And I can tell by the way you're talking that the past isn't letting you go. But there's only so long you can take it all on, then the wrong's gotta be on its own. And

*when you're ready to leave it behind you, you'll look
back and all that you'll see is the wreckage and rust
that you left in the dust on your way to the Jubilee.*

*And I can tell by the way you're listening that you're
still expecting to hear your name being called like a
summons to all who have failed to account for their
doubts and their fears. They can't add up to much without
you and so if it were just up to me I'd take hold of your
hand saying come hear the band play your song at the
Jubilee.*

Mary Chapin Carpenter [19]

'I'm a minister.'

'Oh, really? Which theological college did you go to?'

'Uh . . . I didn't go to theological college.'

'Bible college?'

'No.'

'Are you ordained?'

'Well . . . uh . . . not exactly.'

I could see the look on their face and I could hear
what they were thinking,

'You are not ordained? No Bible training and you
pastor this church? What kind of flaky, illegitimate,
Mickey Mouse church is this?'

And I am thinking to myself, 'Why didn't I go to
theological college? I should have taken university more
seriously. Man, did I screw up my past.'

Rejection. The paralysing experience of disapproval,
repudiation, exclusion and ostracism. Religion has been
good at rejection. Rejection keeps us at arm's length and
stamps us with the label 'loser'. Which should be good

news for you and me, because guess what? Jesus is attracted to losers. Jesus' 'losers' are great candidates for spirituality.

The spirituality of losers

Talk about a loser.

Talk about a moral disaster.

Talk about a person who had made too many mistakes, failed too many times.

Talk about a woman who was a mess. The 'Samaritan woman' in the fourth chapter of John gives new meaning to the word 'mess'.

Divorced five times, when it came to immorality this woman was a pro. Of all the people to bump into the son of God, it had to be a woman whose past suggested she was as far from God as anyone could be.

Surprisingly, Jesus initiates a conversation with her. A respectable Jewish male (especially a respectable Jewish Messiah male) should not be talking to a woman like her, full stop. A woman with her reputation could only damage Jesus' reputation . . . *but he doesn't seem to care!*

Strangely, this woman has studied religion. She knows Messiahs and she definitely knows men, but she's never met a man or a Messiah like this one. This *man* treats her with dignity and respect. What kind of a man is he? He listens to her, converses with her, takes her questions seriously and treats her with dignity and kindness. 'Thank

God,' she thinks, 'at least he doesn't know what kind of woman I am.'

But he *does* know what kind of woman she is.

Turns out *she* doesn't know what kind of woman she is. Jesus brings this woman face to face with herself. She would have done anything to avoid facing who she had become. Jesus knew she couldn't pretend her sin away: she had to face it, look at it, admit it. Jesus knew that in order to get well, she had to get real!

Jesus doesn't lecture, condemn or humiliate. Instead, he gently reminds the woman where her choices have led her. Standing at this unlikely place, her past and her reputation no longer a secret, she admits her deepest longings – her longing for the Messiah. Now she can admit she has waited for him, searched for him, hoped for him. She realises that in her futile search for relationships she was really looking for water – living water. She has spent a lifetime fumbling around for the right man when she was really fumbling around for God. And now he stands before her.

Rather than focusing on her mistakes, *Jesus focuses, instead, on her desire for God*. Jesus recognised her lifetime search for love in all the wrong places and honoured her unsavoury past by looking into her heart instead of looking at her bad choices. Jesus led her to himself.

This woman had truly messed up her life, and Jesus met her in the middle of her mess. No wonder she drops her bucket and runs back into town screaming, 'Come and see a man who told me everything I've ever done!'

Ashamed of her past? Not any more. All she can think about is her future. A woman whose past defined her is now defined by her present. Her muddled, mistake-ridden, sin-cluttered past has driven her to a man like no other man, and she wants everyone to meet him.

When Jesus meets our past

All of the cards are stacked against this woman. Looking at her long string of bad choices, many would consider her unredeemable, unsalvageable, unteachable and beyond help. The woman at the well didn't make a few mistakes, she lived a lifetime of mistakes, enough to cause most to conclude her life was scarred beyond hope, she was incorrigible. She comes to the well at the middle of the day, because respectable women came in the morning and she understands that she is no respectable woman.

But Jesus respects her.

Jesus doesn't see what everyone else sees.

As far as Jesus is concerned, this woman is salvageable, teachable and redeemable. As far as Jesus is concerned, the woman with no future has a future, the woman with a string of failures is about to have the string broken. Jesus sees her present desire which makes her past irrelevant.

You don't suppose, do you, the same could be true for you and me? Our mistakes, our string of failures and what everyone else has labelled unredeemable may actually *be* redeemable? You don't suppose the mess we've made of our lives can be the place where we meet Jesus? Do you?

Our past is a reflection of our longings

Our search for love, for meaning, for happiness, is often our search for God in disguise. When the bottom falls out of our lives, when we come to a dead end, when there is no place to go, we often get in touch with our longings for God. Religion had told the Samaritan woman about the possibility of a Messiah, and she met the real Messiah who immediately recognised her thirst and offered her the living water of his grace. What this woman expected from the Messiah was a lengthy critique, an enlightening lecture on what she should do, a harsh and justifiable reminder of the consequences of her destructive choices on others. What she received instead was compassion, gentleness, kindness and a way out of the ruins of her life.

Jesus went straight for her longings, found them, and in the process found *her*. In a book by New Zealand author Mike Riddell, Vincent has met and fallen in love with a young girl named Marilyn. Neither one of them was seeking a relationship, but a relationship was seeking them. Swept up by their emotions, the two of them become deeply involved. Marilyn, a prostitute, was not prepared to fall in love and was certainly not prepared for the honesty love requires. She must tell Vincent who she is, knowing full well that her painful disclosure will probably mean the end of their relationship.

'Vincent?'

'Mmmm.'

'There's ah . . . there's something we need to talk about.'

'Only if you want to. I'm happy just to sit here and look at you. Sorry, this looks like something serious. Looks a lot like the intro to the Dear John speech, truth be told.'

'It's about me and what I do.'

'Yeah, I wondered when you were going to pluck up the courage to talk about it. Don't tell me, you work for the CIA, right? Sorry, Sorry, I'll shut up.'

She is totally absorbed in the remains of her salad, scrutinising it for something. Anything to avoid his eyes.

'There's no easy way of saying this. I'm a prostitute. I sleep with men for my living. It's a business. I'm very professional.'

Time and silence have this thing they do together. They make a chasm that has no bottom to it. And there you are, standing right on the edge of it. Aware that at any moment you may be falling and falling and falling, with no hope of recovery. At the moment they are at either side of it, each consumed by their private terror. She looks up at last from her salad. Vincent is crying. The tears are streaming down his cheeks, and he is biting his lip to stop himself sobbing.

'I'm sorry. I didn't mean to deceive you. I'm sorry, Vincent. I'm sorry.'

He can't speak. He wants to, but nothing is working. He is looking at her, at her beautiful face, at her eyes, at the slight hardness around her mouth. And weeping and weeping. She reaches a hand across to hold his. She is beyond tears, empty and bleak and barren. Vincent is mumbling something, but is incoherent through the pain. And then he begins to repeat it again and again.

'I love you. I love you. I love you. I love you . . .'

This is the worst thing she has ever heard in her life. She wants to scream, to break something, to tip over the table in rage. Instead some continental shelf rips loose within her. She begins gulping and moaning, a terrible agonising cry from another place. And the tears are flowing. They grip each other's hands and lean their foreheads together. The tears are flowing into the abyss, and there is no end to them.[20]

Marilyn expected Vincent to reject her, to pull away from her, to have nothing to do with her. In a strange and touching way Vincent did what Jesus would do – he looked beneath her behaviour, saw her longings, and all he could do was weep. She expected criticism. What she received instead was *understanding*. Instead of Marilyn hearing words of condemnation, she heard, over and over again, 'I love you.'

The ugliness of rejection

Both Marilyn and the woman at the well were prepared for cold, recriminating condemnation. Based on their experience with religion, these two women were fully expecting judgment and recrimination. Neither one of them was happy with their life choices, neither one of them needed to be reminded of what they had done wrong, neither one of them would have been helped by rubbing salt in their wounds. What they desperately needed, what they desperately wanted, was for someone to recognise what they were looking *for*, not what they were doing. Notice, I did not say they wanted to be legitimised. They weren't looking for someone to condone what they had done, they were looking for someone to accept them. What normally happens with notorious sinners is rejection, distance, separation and withdrawal. Most people don't like sinners, don't want to be around them, and whether they recognise it or not their disdain for the sinner is very clear.

One Sunday morning an older man showed up in our church. His plaited and partially dreadlocked hair hung below his belt, his extremely long frizzy goatee shot in all directions from his chin. He sat in the front row, and his nervousness was obvious. I could feel his fear, it was written all over his being. When it came to the welcome, I talked about how important it is for the church to be a safe place – a place where a few somebodies and mostly nobodies are safe, no matter how unsafe they are outside the church. When we stood up for the giving of the peace, this man mingled throughout our small congregation. After the service he came up to me and said, 'Do you know what it is like to walk into a church and not one person talks to you, not one person touches you and no one even acknowledges your presence? You can feel the rejection. Talk about loneliness.' I could feel the loneliness of this man and I could also feel the pain of knowing his loneliness had been felt and ignored by others.

Without knowing it, he described the woman at the well. She came to the well *alone*. No one wanted to acknowledge her. The visitor to our church was shocked to have been touched, hugged, talked to, acknowledged. It made a deep imprint on him. Which is exactly what happened to the woman at the well.

It is tragic that many of us are afraid to pursue our desire for God because when we have made mistakes and when the scars of our choices are visible others have been quick to isolate us, to distance themselves from us, to condemn our sincerity and our commitment to change either by how we look on the outside or by the reputation that has proceeded us.

The power of the un-changed life

When Jesus had finished talking to the woman at the well, she was just beginning a whole new way of living . . . *but none of the facts of her life had changed.* She was still living with a man who wasn't her husband. She was still divorced five times. Her reputation was still a disaster. Jesus often told people not to talk about their encounters with him – but not this woman. Her faith was only a few minutes old, and already she had become an evangelist, already she was having a huge influence on her community. What did she say? Not much. 'Hey . . . come and see a man who told me everything I've ever done.' Everyone in town knew what this woman had done. Big deal. What she said was *under*whelming. But the fact that she publicly talked about her shameful past was *over*whelming.

Her words were few and seemingly insignificant, but her saying them at all was very significant. In effect she was saying, 'I know you know who I am, but I've just met someone who has liberated me from my past, from my reputation, and I am no longer the person you think I am. I am no longer a hostage to my bad choices. I am *free*. I am free.'

Still, nothing had changed . . . but *everything* had changed. Her neighbours could hear it in her voice and see it in her eyes. Her words were all they needed to race to the man she described. For reasons they didn't understand, who this woman was *now* seemed to be more relevant that who she was *then*.

The implications for us are overwhelming. Those of us who want to move on from our past, those of us who have come to the end of the road, can start with our *un*-changed life, now. We don't have to wait until we are 'mature'. We don't have to move to a new town or convince others we are serious, we simply start. We begin. We take the first bumbling, stumbling, teetering step towards the spiritual life . . . *even if we're not very good at it.*

Little League baseball can be a brutal sport for children, especially for nine- and ten-year-olds who compete in national competitions.

It was the area Little League championship game. The stands were packed full with families of each of the players. One young man brought his mother and father, both grandparents and three uncles and aunts to watch him play.

The bottom of the seventh innings was a nail-biter. The other team was ahead by one run, the bases were loaded, two out, and the little boy with the large family was up to bat. If he made an out, the game would be over and his team would lose. If he walked or hit the ball, he would be the hero of the game.

The first pitch was swung at and missed. 'Strike one!' the umpire yelled. The families from the other teams cheered, but his family cheered even louder, 'It's okay, Carl. No problem. You almost hit the ball! Now, clobber the next pitch!'

'Strike twoooo!' the umpire yelled after the next pitch.

Pandemonium broke out. Both teams and their families were yelling back and forth to each other, Carl's family and team were encouraging him, the players and family of the defensive team were taunting. No one could hear themselves think. Wrinkles appeared on Carl's nine-year-old forehead as he waited for the next pitch. The ball left the pitcher's hand and everything went very quiet as it sped towards Carl. It seemed to take for ever to cross the plate, but cross the plate it did, and Carl swung with all his might.

But he missed.

'Strike three!!! YOU'RE OUT!'

Not only was Carl out, the game was over and he was the cause of the loss.

The winning team went crazy, their family members swarmed on to the field and everyone was dancing, laughing, cheering and celebrating. But not Carl's team. As Carl's team members walked dejectedly off the field, they mingled with their families and headed back to their cars in silence.

Except for Carl.

Carl was still standing at the plate, devastated, alone, his head down, in disgrace. Suddenly someone yelled, 'Okay, Carl, play ball!' Startled, Carl looked up to see his family spread out over the field. Grandpa was pitching, Dad was catching, Mum was at first base, Uncle David was at second and the rest of the family had covered the other positions.

'Come on, Carl, pick up the bat. Grandpa's pitching.' Bewildered, Carl slowly picked up the bat and swung at Grandpa's first pitch. He missed, and missed the next six pitches as well. But on the seventh pitch, determined to hit the ball, Carl smacked the ball to left field. His aunt ran, picked up the ball and threw it to first base in plenty of time, but the first baseman – Mum – must have lost the ball in the sun because she let the ball go right through her hands into the dugout behind. 'RUN!' everyone yelled. As Carl was running to second, the first baseman recovered the ball and threw it towards the second baseman. Amazingly, Uncle David was blinded by the sun as well. 'Keep running!' yelled someone, and Carl headed for third base where the throw went at least two feet over the head of the baseman. 'Keep running, Carl!' And Carl raced for home, running as hard as he had ever run. The ball was thrown with dead accuracy as the catcher, blocking home plate, waited to tag out the runner, but just as Carl and the ball reached home plate, the ball bounced in and out of the catcher's mitt and Carl was safe!

Before Carl knew what was happening, he found himself being carried around on Uncle David's shoulders while the rest of the family crowded round, cheering his name.

One person who was watching this amazing event commented to a friend, 'I watched a little boy fall victim to a *conspiracy of grace!*'

Carl, the loser. Carl, the one who struck out, failed his team, disappointed his family, went from loser to hero. Carl, who would have been left with the awful memory of his past failures, was instead given a memory of grace, love and acceptance.

Just like a certain women at a well.

I know about conspiracies of grace. I have been the victim of one myself.

At the beginning of the chapter I pointed out my lack of training as a minister, my unordained status, which, if I'm honest, has bothered me as much as it bothers others. My uneducated past haunts me.

Two years ago I was invited to speak at the Oregon Seventh-Day Adventists annual ministers' retreat. Over 150 ministers from the state of Oregon attended. I am not a Seventh-Day Adventist, but I have always considered Adventists brothers and sisters in Christ, even though I disagree with some of their doctrines. I was invited to speak about the need for youth ministry, allowing both the Adventists and myself to relax about any differences we might have.

In the process of talking about youth, I found myself describing the frustrations of the pastorate, and noticed how many of the ministers were resonating with my thoughts about the Church. Midway through my talks, I abandoned my youth ministry remarks and talked about the loneliness and struggles of the pastorate. I referred many times to my lack of ordination, and yet I noticed how well we connected, even to the point of tears for some of the ministers.

After I had finished my final talk, the leaders came forward and asked me to stay. They had a gift for me. I had a good idea what my gift would be – a t-shirt, which is the gift of choice for most conferences. But was I wrong!

The state director began, 'Mike, you have spent the entire weekend apologising for your lack of training. You have constantly referred to yourself as a 'mail-order minister' and reminded us you weren't a real minister because you aren't ordained. Well, you are wrong, Mike, because you have ministered to us this week. We think you are a real minister. While you've been speaking, we've been in contact with our national headquarters. As far as we know, this has never been done before, but we want to ordain you in the Seventh-Day Adventist Church!'

The entire room sat in stunned silence. People looked shocked at first, then hesitant, and suddenly everyone was on their feet walking towards the front of the room. One hundred and fifty ministers laid hands on me and ordained me into the Seventh-Day Adventist Church.

After the service, no one knew how to respond or how to explain what had just happened. But I knew what had happened. Jesus was in the building. I think Jesus was tired of my whining, tired of hearing me question my calling, so he decided to shut me up for good. I could just see him smiling, 'Okay, are you happy? Now you are ordained, so shut up already.'

Of course, I went back to my church and told them I had good news and bad news. I was now ordained, but we were meeting on Saturdays!

Jesus can redeem our past, no matter what kind of past we bring with us: failure, mistakes, bad decisions, immaturity – and even a past which was done to us.

When our past was done to us

Not everyone has chosen their past. Too many carry the scars of physical, mental or psychological abuse, awakening each day to the haunting memories of a time when they were acted upon, against their will, and now find themselves hopelessly trapped between facing their past and running from it. A sad reality of modern life is the increasing number of people whose past abuse has convinced them of their unworthiness. Often it is the abused who have decided they are disqualified from the possibility of God's grace. The abused see themselves as damaged beyond repair, soiled goods which cannot be cleaned, prisoners who cannot be free.

Evangelist Rich Wilkerson held a large crusade in the west of the United States. Many hundreds came forward that night, too many for Rich to meet individually. A few weeks after the crusade, however, he received a letter:

Dear Mr Wilkerson

I attended your crusade in Seattle a few weeks ago. It's my first year of college and a group of my friends invited me to come to your crusade. I agreed, reluctantly, but I was desperate. The preceding four years before college were the worst years of my life and I was willing to try anything that might help. My nightmare started when I turned fourteen. That was the year my uncle moved into our home. Shortly after he moved in, he would sneak into my bedroom and sexually abuse me. He threatened to hurt me if I told anyone, so I endured the abuse, saying nothing, anxiously awaiting my first year of college when I would be out of the house.

By the time I entered college, I was a mess. My first year was a disaster. I slept with any guy who would have me, drank and drugged myself into forgetfulness almost every night, but I would still be awakened by nightmares. When I came to your crusade I was at breaking point, and when you asked us to come forward to meet Jesus, I almost ran to the front.

On the five-hour drive home, I fell asleep. I dreamed I was asleep in my college room when I was awakened by my uncle once again. I wanted to scream for help or get out of bed and run, but I could do neither. He kept asking me to come to him, and I could not resist. I could feel myself giving up and coming to him once again, when suddenly the door to my room opened again. It was Jesus, with his arms wide open, beckoning me to come to him. I jumped out of bed and ran past my uncle into the arms of Jesus. I woke up with all the girls in the car looking at me because I was crying, saying out loud, 'I'm free! I'm free! I'm really free.'[21]

The freedom of the present

A young college girl with a past meets the Jesus of the present. As with the woman at the well, nothing had changed and everything had changed. Abuse was still part of her past, but hope was now part of her present. I can see her saying to her friends, 'Come and see a man who liberated me from my past.' As messy as this woman's past was, she was now free to seek the spiritual life.

Odd Discipleship

The consequence of lopsided spirituality

Vocation does not mean a goal that I pursue. It means a calling that I hear. Before I can tell my life what I want to do with it, I must listen to my life telling me who I am.

Parker Palmer[22]

When artists discover as children that they have inappropriate responses to events around them, they also find, as they learn to trust those responses, that these oddities are what constitute their value to others.

Kathleen Norris[23]

He got all As and flunked life.

Walker Percy[24]

It is not going to be easy to listen to God's call. Your insecurity, your self-doubt and your great need for affirmation make you lose trust in your inner voice and

run away from yourself. But you know that God speaks
to you through your inner voice and that you will find
joy and peace only if you follow it.

Henri Nouwen[25]

One of my favourite stories is about a boy named
Norman in Robert Fulghum's book, *Uh-Oh*.

Remember in primary school when the teacher
would announce the spring play? Everyone's hand would
shoot into the air volunteering to be one of the
characters. Of course, the choice characters would be
decided first.

In Fulghum's story, Norman's teacher announced the
play for the year – *Cinderella*. Chaos ensued as a sea of
arms waved wildly, each child trying to get the teacher's
attention. 'I want to be Cinderella,' every girl yelled. 'I
want to be the handsome prince!' the boys shouted.
Realising everyone couldn't have just these two roles,
the kids soon erupted into urgent requests for other parts:
'I want to be the wicked stepmother!' 'I want to be an
ugly sister!' Somehow the teacher was able to wade
through all the requests, and soon everyone was assigned
at least one part.

Except for Norman. Norman was a quiet young man
who didn't talk much in class. He wasn't shy or bashful;
he just didn't feel like talking a lot of the time. Talking
about nothing was a waste of time to Norman. He only
talked when he had something to say. Norman had a
mind of his own and was perfectly comfortable just being
himself. As the teacher looked over her cast of characters,

she realised Norman didn't have a role. Concerned because there weren't any more characters in *Cinderella* (even though she had made up many 'extra' parts) and knowing Norman very well, she said, 'Norman, I'm afraid all the main parts have been taken for Cinderella, but I'm sure we can find an extra part for you. What character would you like to be?'

Norman did not hesitate. 'I would like to be the pig,' he declared.

'Pig?' the teacher said, bewildered. 'But there is no pig in Cinderella.'

Norman smiled and said, 'There is now.'

Norman designed his own costume – a paper cup for a nose, and pink long underwear with a pipe-cleaner tail. His pig followed Cinderella wherever she went and became a mirror of the action on stage. If Cinderella was happy, the pig was happy; if Cinderella was sad, the pig was sad. One look at Norman and you knew the emotions of the moment. At the end of the play, when the handsome prince placed the glass slipper on Cinderella's foot and the couple hugged and ran off happily together . . .

Norman went wild with joy, danced around on his hind legs, and broke his silence by barking. In rehearsal, the teacher had tried explaining to Norman that even if there was a pig in *Cinderella*, pigs don't bark. But as she expected, Norman explained that *this* pig barked. And the barking, she had to admit, *was* well done. The presentation at the teachers' conference was a smash hit. At the curtain call, guess who received a standing ovation? Of course, Norman the barking pig. Who was, after all, the *real* Cinderella story.[26]

What I love about the story is the strong-willed stubbornness of Norman. Impervious to intimidation, resistant to the limited categories of the official script, Norman refused to believe he had no place. Rather than the script limiting him, Norman found a way to enhance it, to fill it full of life and laughter and surprise.

Norman was so like Jesus. The religious leaders of the day had written the script for the Messiah. When Jesus announced *he* was the Messiah, the Pharisees and others screamed to him, 'There is no Jesus in the "Messiah" script. Messiahs do not hang out with losers. Our Messiah does not break all the rules. Our Messiah does not question our leadership, or threaten our religion, or act so irresponsibly. Our Messiah does not disregard his reputation, befriend ordinary common riffraff, nor frequent the questionable haunts of questionable people.'

Jesus' reply? *This* Messiah *does*!

Do you see why Christianity is called 'good news'? It proclaims to all of us that Christianity is an equal-opportunity faith, open to all, in spite of the abundance of playwrights in the church who are more than anxious to announce, 'There is no place for you in Christianity if you . . . [wear an ear-ring/have a tattoo/drink wine/have too many questions/look weird/smoke/dance/haven't been "filled with the Spirit"/aren't baptised/swear/have pink hair/are in the wrong ethnic group/have a nose ring/have had an abortion/are gay or lesbian/are too conservative or too liberal . . .].'

Jesus believed Messiahs find places for those who have *no* place, and as a result he invited every 'Norman' he could find to his place – from sleazy businessmen, terrorists, dockworkers, bully tax collectors, dangerous psychotics and hopelessly deranged outcasts, to the successful, rich and overprivileged elite of society. The Christianity of Jesus became the 'place-maker' for those who had no place.

The gift of oddness

When Jesus is around 'no place' is a great place because our out-of-place-ness is exactly the place where our spiritual life begins.

Well, not exactly.

What characterises Christianity in the modern world is its oddness. Christianity is home for people who are out of step, unfashionable, unconventional and counter-cultural. As Peter says, 'strangers and aliens'.

Churches are not glistening cathedrals filled exclusively with beautiful Cinderellas. Churches are noisy rollicking madhouses filled with yelping, dancing, barking pigs who follow the *real* Cinderella wherever he goes. Churches are not only awe-inspiring, they are *odd*-inspiring, attracting an earthy assortment of Jesus' followers. The stained glass is extraordinary, but it is also covered with 'ordinary' fingerprints at the same time. Dirt from the fields is scattered on the glistening marble sanctuary floors. Sprinkled throughout the cathedral of Christ is the heavenly smell of incense mingled with the 'piggy' fragrance of sweaty, commonplace, messy disciples.

I pastor the slowest-growing church in America. We started twelve years ago with ninety members and have un-grown to thirty. We are about as far as you can get from a 'user-friendly' church – not because our congregation is unfriendly, but because our services are unpredictable, unpolished and inconsistent. We are an 'odd-friendly' church, attracting unique and different followers of Christ who make every service a surprise.

One Sunday morning, one of our parishioners forgot that she was to read the Scripture. When it was time for the reading, there was a long, awkward moment of silence. Conscious that something was awry, the woman looked up and realised everyone was staring at her. Shocked and embarrassed at her lapse of memory, she blurted out loudly, 'Sh–t!' A long period of silence followed, and then the laughter began. It was the strangest call to the reading of the Gospel I have ever experienced. The woman was embarrassed, apologised and went on to read the Scripture. I am certainly not condoning the use of swear words in church, but it *was* an accident, it *was* funny and, we had to admit, she read the Scripture with a humility and a vigour that our church hadn't seen in years.

Such happenings are not unusual in our church because we refuse to edit oddness and incompetence from our services. We believe our oddness matters. We want our services filled with mistakes and surprises, because life is full of mistakes and surprises. One Sunday morning, during the time for prayer requests, a member began describing the critical illness of her father. Because she was close to her father her request for prayer was frequently interrupted by tears. Those around her reached out a hand or nodded with sadness. Some found their eyes filling with tears as well. The woman finished her request as best as she could. Seated in the front row was Sadie – the young woman with Down's Syndrome you read about earlier. Sadie stood and walked up the aisle until she saw the woman in the middle of her row. Stepping over the feet of other people in the aisle, Sadie reached the woman, bent down on her knees, laid her head on the woman's lap and cried with her. Sadie 'inconvenienced' an entire row of people, stepped on their shoes and forced them to make room for her ... but none of us will ever forget that moment. Sadie is *still* teaching the rest of us what the odd compassion of Christ's Church looks like.

Odd vs same

Someone said, 'You shall know the truth and the truth shall make you odd'. Whoever made that statement understood what it means to be a follower of Christ.

Followers of Christ are odd. Oddness is important because it is the quality that adds colour, texture, variety, beauty to the human condition. Christ doesn't make us the same. What he does is *affirm our differentness*. Oddness is important because the most dangerous word in Western culture is 'sameness'. Sameness is a virus that infects members of industrialised nations and causes an allergic reaction to anyone who is different. This virus affects the decision-making part of our brain, resulting in an obsession with making the identical choices that everyone else is making.

Sameness is a disease with disastrous consequences – differences are ignored, uniqueness is not listened to, our gifts are cancelled out, and the place where life, passion and joy reside is snuffed out. Sameness is the result of sin. Sin does much more than infect us with lust and greed: it flattens the human race, enslaves us, attempts to make us all homogeneous. Sameness is the cemetery where our distinctiveness dies. In a sea of sameness, no one has an identity. But Christians do have an identity – aliens! We are the odd ones, the strange ones, the misfits, the outsiders, the incompatibles. Oddness is a gift of God and sits dormant until God's Spirit gives it life and shape. Oddness is the consequence of following the One who made us unique, different . . . and *in his image!*

For God so loved the world, that whosoever believes in him will, from that point on, be considered weird by the rest of the world, which means the Church should be more like a zoo than a tomb of identical mummies.

In C. S. Lewis's *The Lion, the Witch and the Wardrobe,* the White Witch has turned many of the inhabitants of Narnia into stone when Aslan, the Christ figure, jumps into the stone courtyard, pouncing on the statues and breathing life into them.

Creatures were running after Aslan and dancing round him till he was almost hidden in the crowd. Instead of all that deadly white, the courtyard was now a blaze of colours; glossy chestnut sides of centaurs, indigo horns of unicorns, dazzling plumage of birds, reddy-brown of foxes, dogs and satyrs, yellow stockings and crimson hoods of dwarfs; and the birch-girls in silver, and the beech-girls in fresh, transparent green, and the larch-girls in green so bright that it was almost yellow. And instead of the deadly silence, the whole place rang with the sound of happy roarings, brayings, yelpings, barkings, squealings, cooings, neighings, stampings, shouts, hurrahs, songs and laughter.[27]

Lewis summarises what is happening in Narnia with a brilliant description of what the Church *should* look like. 'The courtyard looked no longer like a museum; it looked more like a zoo.'[28] It is the zoo-like incongruency and the oddness of our disjointed spirituality that ought to characterise every church.

Unbalanced

Balance is a cherished value in modern society. Balance means that there are no extremes and that every negative is offset by an equal but opposite positive. Balance is a condition of neutrality, where the middle is considered desirable and healthy. When someone is described as 'balanced' it is understood as a compliment, implying that the person is well adjusted, sensible and stable. 'Balanced' describes a person who moderates all aspects of their life, physical, mental, social and spiritual, and has found the perfect mix of all these attributes. Balance *sounds* like a characteristic of the Christian faith, like a goal to seek after and a quality worth cultivating. Balance *sounds* like a worthy ideal, a perfect description of a healthy follower of Christ.

Beware of balance.

Balance is a dangerous, illusionary characteristic and a seductive temptress. Disguised as normal and sensible, it is silently destructive, crushing the unbalance of giftedness, taming the extremes of passion, snuffing out the raging fire of a genuine relationship with Jesus. Jesus and his disciples were constantly criticised for being unbalanced. Think about it: Jesus could have healed six days a week and not upset anyone. People would have been just as healed on the second day of the week as they were on the Sabbath. Jesus could have sat down with the temple leaders and quietly discussed his theological reasoning for not allowing the place of worship to become a carnival of commerce. Instead, he crashed in like a crazy man with a whip and knocked over the tables, screaming and yelling and creating total chaos. He certainly could have been more 'balanced'.

In the book of Matthew, Jesus warns what happens when you decide to be his disciple. His description of discipleship is a virtual *manual* of unbalance.

Discipleship creates tension in families, can bring about financial ruin or questionable reputations. It sometimes makes enemies instead of friends, and nomads instead of solid stable citizens (see Matthew 10:5–42). Jesus warned that the witness of our faith is the perception by most that we are unbalanced, unstable, scary people to be around.

Think about how many of us have wondered why we don't fit, why our faith doesn't stabilise us, why we seem so out of sync with most of the world. Genuine faith is the isolating force in our lives that creates tension wherever we go. To put it another way, faith is the unbalancing force in our life that is the fruit of God's disturbing presence in our lives.

One Sunday morning in our church, the pastor (that would be me) *and* the communion co-ordinator forgot that it was communion Sunday. During the middle of my sermon, the woman responsible for the communion table remembered. She looked at me and panicked, looked around the room trying to think of what to do, stood up and left the meeting room and disappeared into the kitchen. I was still preaching. A few minutes later, she reappeared with the wine and the bread, set up the table in front of me (I was still trying to preach) and sat down. I finished the sermon, finally, and moved into the communion service. I began with the words about the breaking of the bread: 'On the night Jesus was betrayed, he took bread . . .' I reached down, uncovering the bread, and there, in plain view, was our communion loaf . . . *hot dog buns!* The woman in charge of communion was not afraid to admit she had forgotten communion, she was not concerned about disrupting the service and, most of all, she did not want to put communion off to another week. She *loves* communion, so she improvised from the meagre stock in the kitchen. Her love of Christ drove her to risk being thought of as 'disruptive' so we could celebrate what our church is *really* about – the body and blood of Jesus. Of course, she also gave us the most unusual communion service we've ever experienced and a memory none of us will never forget, which is what happens when we allow people to express their uniqueness – warm memories and godly surprises abound.

A number of years ago, a group of adults and high school students from our church travelled to Mexico to build houses. Most truck rental companies won't let you take their vehicles into Mexico because moving trucks are easily stolen, but because we live in a small town the owner of the local truck rental company agreed to let us take a vehicle into Mexico. He trusted us – after all, we were building houses for Jesus. We filled our rented truck with clothes, building supplies, tents, food and tools.

Once we crossed the border into Mexico, we headed for the toll road between Tijuana and Ensenada. After paying the toll, we noticed a group of federal police parked on the side of the road, and as we passed them we were waved over by three tough-looking young policemen, each holding a large machine-gun. The policemen walked up to our truck and asked me to step out of the cab. Standing in front of them, I could not believe how big and menacing those machine-guns looked. The officer in the middle spoke in Spanish. One of our group members translated his short speech: 'We are taking your truck. Please move out of the way.' We pleaded with the police officer in the middle not to confiscate our truck, explaining that we were building houses for the poor and we were doing this for Jesus. The more we talked, the more angry and demanding the officer became.

Suddenly one of the young people, a sixteen-year-old foreign exchange student from Chile, interrupted the conversation. Politely but firmly, I took the young man aside and explained to him the seriousness of the situation. 'Look,' I said, 'I know you want to help, but these soldiers are angry and those machine-guns look pretty convincing.'

'Oh, I've seen lots of machine-guns in our country,' he replied confidently, unruffled by my warning. Before I could stop him, he grabbed the rental contract, walked over to the men and began yelling at the officer in the middle, waving his hands and frantically pointing to the contract. Then he actually pushed his finger into the soldier's chest.

I thought, *This is it – we're all headed for a Mexican jail.*

But the more the boy yelled, the more sheepish the federal guardsman looked, until, exasperated, he stopped the boy with a loud '*VAMOS!*' Immediately the boy turned to me and said, 'Get in the truck. Let's get out of here before he changes his mind.' We jumped into the truck and drove off in a cloud of dust.

As we fled the scene I asked this young exchange student what he'd said to the guard that made him change his mind.

'I pointed to the contract and told him it said the truck was legal in Mexico and that he would be in a lot of trouble if we lost it,' he replied happily.

'But the contract doesn't say that,' I objected.

'I know, but the officer couldn't read English!' he told me.

Now, the young Chilean didn't act very spiritually – he lied! His spirituality certainly didn't look like spirituality. Our pursuit of spirituality is not always nice, nor is it sanitised. It often gets messy, landing more outside the lines than we think.

God likes odd people

It's difficult to be odd in a culture of sameness. Society is not kind to the odd, the strange, the different, the broken and the outcasts. But Jesus is. Sophisticated culture doesn't like aliens and rejects. But Jesus likes us. Most people would not choose odd people, but Jesus chooses us.

I wonder how many of us have turned away from Jesus, given up any hope of the spiritual life because we don't fit, because we aren't like everyone else, and because our Christianity seems so different and strange from the rest of the Church? I wonder if we realise how anxious Jesus is to reach out and walk with us arm in arm?

In Daniel Taylor's marvellous book *Letters To My Children*, he describes an experience he had in his last year of primary school. Periodically the students were taught how to dance. Thank God this kind of thing isn't done any more, but then the teacher would line up the boys at the door of the classroom to choose their partner. Imagine what it would have been like to be one of the girls waiting to be chosen, wondering if they were going to be chosen, wondering if they would be chosen by someone they didn't like. One girl, Mary, was always chosen last. Because of a childhood illness, one of her arms was drawn up and she had a bad leg. She wasn't pretty, she wasn't clever and she was . . . well . . . fat. The teacher's assistant for Dan's class happened to attend his church. One day, she pulled him to one side and said, 'Dan, next time we have dancing, I want you to choose Mary.' Dan couldn't believe it. Why would anyone pick Mary when there was Linda, Shelley or even Doreen? But Dan's teacher told him that it was what Jesus would have done, and deep inside he knew she was right –

which didn't make it any easier. All Dan could hope for was that he would be last in line. That way, he could choose Mary, do the right thing, and no one would be any the wiser. Instead, he was first in line.

The faces of the girls were turned towards me, some smiling. I looked at Mary and saw that she was only half-turned to the back of the room. (She knew no one would pick her first) . . . Mr Jenkins said, 'Okay, Dan – choose your partner!'

I remember feeling very far away. I heard my voice say, 'I choose Mary.'

Never has reluctant virtue been so rewarded. I still see her face undimmed in my memory. She lifted her head, and on her face, reddened with pleasure and surprise and embarrassment all at once, was the most genuine look of delight and even pride that I have ever seen, before or since. It was so pure that I had to look away because I knew I didn't deserve it.

Mary came and took my arm, as we had been instructed, and she walked beside me, bad leg and all, just like a princess . . .

Mary is my age now. I never saw her after that year. I don't know what her life's been like or what she's doing. But I'd like to think she has a fond memory of at least one day in sixth grade.

I know I do.[29]

There was nothing Mary could do. She was chosen, and she was chosen *first*. I have the feeling all of heaven stood and applauded not only Mary but all of the barking pigs out there who have decided to call themselves Christians. And when others say, 'Christians don't act like you!' we respond, 'Well, they do *now*.'

Unspiritual Growth

Unprinciples of erratic discipleship

Dear God.
I think about you sometimes even when I'm not praying.
Elliott[30]

The church, by and large, has had a poor record of
encouraging freedom. She has spent so much time
inculcating in us the fear of making mistakes that she
has made us like ill-taught piano students: we play our
songs, but we never really hear them because our main
concern is not to make music but to avoid some flub that
will get us in dutch.

Robert Capon[31]

Man has set out at tremendous speed . . . to go nowhere.
Jacques Ellul[32]

A woman described her dark night to me. 'It's as if God
lifted the lid of a music box in a dark room inside of me

99

and then vanished. It's a beautiful turn, a new sound:
and hearing it, I can't forget it. I'm like a child leaving
my nursery, stumbling through a dark house in search of
the Music Maker.

Sue Monk Kidd[33]

I don't believe in spiritual growth.

Maybe I should clarify.

I don't believe in what most people *mean* by spiritual growth. Spiritual growth has become an industry, a system, a set of principles, formulas, training programmes, curricula, books and tapes, which, if followed, promise to produce maturity and depth. Most of these programmes are made up of the same ingredients: prayer, Bible study, service and community. Duh. Authentic growth doesn't happen overnight. It can't be reduced to a formula (*take some verses, wash down with a couple of prayers, and call me in the morning*).

Yes, a regimen of prayer, Bible study, service and community can and will contribute to spiritual growth, but that's like saying that milk, vegetables and chicken will contribute to my physical growth. Physical and spiritual growth cannot be reduced to mechanics. I'm all for getting the mechanics right, but spiritual growth is more than a procedure; it's a wild search for God in the midst of the tangled jungle of our souls, a search which involves a volatile mix of messy reality, wild freedom, frustrating stuckness, increasing slowness and a healthy dose of gratitude.

Now are you ready to talk about spiritual growth?

The kind of spiritual growth that begins with desire, not guilt; passion, not principles; desperation, not obligation? Are you ready to grow by travelling the road of failure, frustration and surprise?

Let's get started.

In his book *The Easy Yoke*,[34] Doug Webster tells a story about a young idealistic college student who ended up on a mission trip to one of the more dangerous housing projects in Philadelphia. A brand-new Christian, this wide-eyed urban missionary didn't have a clue about how to evangelise the inner city. Frightened and anxious to share his new faith, the young man approached a very large tenement house. Cautiously making his way through the dark cluttered hallways, he gingerly climbed up one flight of stairs to an apartment. He knocked on the door, and a woman holding a naked howling baby opened it. She was smoking and not in any mood to hear some white idealistic college boy tell her about Jesus. She started cursing him and slammed the door in his face. The young man felt devastated.

He walked out to the street, sat on the curb and wept. 'Look at me ... how in the world could someone like me think I could tell anyone about Jesus?' Then he remembered that the baby was naked and the woman was smoking. The plan forming in his head didn't seem terribly *spiritual*, but . . .

He ran down the street to the local market and bought a box of nappies and a pack of cigarettes. When he knocked on the door again, he showed the woman his purchases. She hesitated and then invited him in. For the rest of the day he played with the baby and changed its nappies (even though he had never changed nappies before). When the woman offered him a cigarette, even though he didn't smoke he smoked. He spent the entire day smoking and changing nappies. Never said a word about Jesus. Late in the afternoon the woman asked him why he was doing all this, and finally he got to tell her everything he knew about Jesus. Took about five minutes. When he stopped talking, the woman looked at him and said softly, 'Pray for me and my baby that we can make it out of here alive,' so he did.

This young college boy received a lesson in spiritual growth. In one frustrating afternoon, he learned about the power of sensitivity, the meaning of evangelism, the hopelessness of those who live in urban areas. He also learned that sometimes the Holy Spirit asks us to violate our own convictions *for a season* in order to live the faith, not just talk about it. When this young man returned to college he didn't start smoking, but he did start listening to the leading of the Holy Spirit. What an education! What a growth-producing experiment.

Can you imagine this young man standing in front of his congregation talking about his new programme of smoking evangelism? It certainly would be an interesting evening. Doesn't sound very different from the day Jesus let a woman waste a bottle of expensive perfume on him. I have the feeling there was a spiritual growth going on around the dinner table that night.

Messy reality

One look at the book of Corinthians and it's clear the Christian life doesn't take place in the rarefied air of perfection. Paul wrote his letter to the church at Corinth to help them figure out what Christianity means in the everyday-ness of life. Paul gives us spectacular glimpses of Jesus while trying to explain what he looks like in the midst of incestuous affairs, vicious lawsuits, divorce and separation, idol worship, over-inflated egos, doctrinal infighting, jealousy, sexual promiscuity and getting drunk during communion. And that was just one small congregation! Spiritual growth thrives in the midst of our problems, not in their absence. Spiritual growth occurs in the trenches of life, not in the classroom.

We don't grow while studying the definition of consistency, we grow when we try to *be* consistent in a inconsistent world. We can talk about love all we want, but loving those who are unlovely is the place we learn about love. Jesus gave Peter some excellent teaching about betrayal and arrogance, but Peter didn't understand what Jesus was talking about *until he actually betrayed Jesus*. Peter's failure was the primary cause of his understanding and maturity.

So do we encourage people to fail so they can grow? No, we encourage people to grow, which means they will fail. We encourage each other to keep our eyes on Jesus, but we are not paranoid about failure. Paul himself said, 'I am not saying that I have this all together, that I have it made. But I am well on my way, reaching out for Christ, who has so wondrously reached out for me. Friends, don't get me wrong; by no means am I an expert in all of this, but I've got my eye on the goal, where God is beckoning us onwards – to Jesus. I'm off and running, and I'm not turning back.'

Wild freedom

Freedom in Christ. What a nice concept. Sadly, most Christians are frightened of freedom. Ever since Jesus announced, 'You shall know the truth and the truth will set you free,' many in the Church have tried to explain away his remarks by saying, 'What Jesus meant is that we are free not to sin.' Which is true. We are free not to sin . . . and we are also free to sin.

The radical truth of freedom in Christ is that I am free to choose good or bad, right or wrong, this way or that way. I can choose to run *to* Christ or to run *away from* Christ. Freedom in Christ means I am free from everyone else's definition of freedom for me. Because I am free in Christ, Christ is the only one I answer to. Because I am free in Christ, I am free from other people's concern that I might not use my freedom well. Paul said in 2 Corinthians 3:17, 'and where the Spirit of the Lord is, there is freedom'.

The psalmist said, 'I will walk about in freedom for I have sought out your precepts.' Freedom is clearly connected to 'seeking out your precepts', which means that those who seek to follow God's commands are set free to roam in the wide open spaces of his love.

God's word makes it clear he trusts us with freedom, even though it can be misused, even though he knows we might not be able to handle freedom. All he can do is leave us with his words, his precepts, and then let us figure out how a spiritual person would act in the context of our lives.

Frustrating stuckness

I would like to add two words to our vocabulary of spiritual growth: 'stuck' and 'unstuck'. Most Christians consider being 'stuck' a sign of failure or burn-out, an indication that a person isn't working hard enough on their spiritual life. Being stuck means getting an 'F' on our spiritual school report. The hidden assumption is, 'if you are stuck in your spiritual life, you aren't doing something right, because dedicated Christians should *never* be stuck'.

Nothing could be more untrue.

Actually, *getting stuck is the prerequisite to getting unstuck.*

Getting stuck is a great moment, a summons, a call from within, the glorious music of disaffection and dissatisfaction with our current place in life. We get stuck when we want to change, but can't; when we want to stop destructive behaviour, but don't; when the tug-o-war between God's will and ours stands still and we can't move. We're stuck going nowhere, unable to get beyond a particular point.

Getting stuck can be the best thing that could happen to us, because it forces us to stop. It halts the momentum of our lives; we have no choice but to notice what is around us – and we end up searching for Jesus. When we're stuck, we're much more likely to pay attention to our hunger for God and the longings and yearnings we have stifled. Sometimes being stuck is the final low point and we say, 'Okay, I give up.' We cannot grow without first giving up and letting go. Getting stuck forces us to see the futility of our situation and to put life in perspective so that we can move on.

One summer day, our company staff was scheduled to participate in a ropes course. We had decided that we needed an experience that would bring our employees together and encourage us to work as a team. We had signed up to participate in both the low and the high courses.

Looming before all of us was the Centurion, a hundred-foot-high challenge. After climbing the tiniest of metal steps hammered into the side of a tree, you reached 'the plank', a small platform that narrowed to a six-foot length of a 2×12 board. Standing on the end of the plank you could look a hundred feet down into what appeared to be an endless abyss. About six feet away from the tip of the plank was a trapeze. The challenge was to leap from the plank and catch the trapeze with your hands like a circus performer.

My fear of heights has increased with age, and I

decided early in the day not to attempt the Centurion. One of the ropes course staff kept stopping off to talk to me during the day, challenging me: 'Come on, you can do the Centurion. I'll help you. I know you can do it.' Now the sun was beginning to set and we had approximately fifteen minutes before we headed home. The young staff member persisted, 'Let's go. I know you can do it. If you don't try, you'll regret it.'

His persistence paid off. I decided to tackle the Centurion. I began my slow ascent to the top of the tree. It seemed like hours before I reached the top, and when I did everyone on the ground looked like ants. I was petrified. I sat on the plank, stuck. I could not move. But the longer I sat on the plank, the calmer I became, and my resolve started to build. After at least ten minutes of stuckness, I got to my feet, walked briskly to the end of the plank, hesitated a few seconds – *and jumped*.

I will never forget the exhilaration I felt as my hands grasped the trapeze and I swung back and forth. I was laughing uncontrollably and I didn't want to let go. Finally, I let the belayer slowly lower me back to earth. I had been stuck all day, and even once I had decided to climb the Centurion I remained stuck on the plank, afraid to move. But my stuckness was preparing me for the jump. While I was stuck, my mind was carrying on a dialogue with my fears, and after a lengthy discussion my fears lost. I was ready to jump, and I did.

I don't know if words can explain what happened to me, but something inside me changed. My fear of heights was lessened somewhat but, more important, other obstacles in my life – decisions I had been procrastinating over making – suddenly were less intimidating. My entire day of paralysing stuckness had resulted in a new confidence, a new courage to face the fears which had been plaguing me.

There are other kinds of stuckness, of course. Like the quagmire of belief or the quicksand of doubt. Years ago I heard an extraordinary story. I hope it's true. The pastor of a church in England announced to his congregation one Sunday that he was resigning because he no longer believed in Christianity. Stunned at first, the congregation slowly gathered its composure, and the elders asked the pastor to a meeting with the entire congregation after the service. Everyone knew what was going to happen. His resignation would be accepted, financial arrangements would be made, and the search for a new pastor would begin.

But that is not what happened.

The elders stood before the pastor and said, 'Sir, we understand you have come to the painful conclusion that Christianity is not true. We believe it *is* true. In fact, we're so convinced it is true, we want you to stay on as our pastor. We want you to stand up each Sunday and preach your doubts to us. It's okay. We want to hear them, not so we can argue with you, but for this to be a place where you can honestly seek the truth.'

For three years the pastor preached his doubts – and one morning he stood in the pulpit, looked out at the congregation with his eyes full of tears, and said, 'I have found my faith again. Thank you for trusting the gospel, thank you for waiting for me to find my faith again!'

This pastor was stuck, burned out, lost, sinking in the quicksand of doubt, and his church *recognised his stuckness!* His congregation recognised that being stuck was a necessary stopping place where he could regroup, regain his strength and move on. An extraordinary congregation of ordinary people understood their pastor's need to wrestle with the truth. Instead of talking about truth, they *trusted* the truth. They did not fear the waiting, nor did they fret over the 'setbacks' they would have to endure when visitors came.

When the doubting pastor finally proclaimed his found-again faith, deep in his heart he must have whispered to God in gratitude, 'Jesus has been hiding in these people all along.'

Increasing slowness

When my children were young, athletics meetings filled part of each week during the spring. One particularly hot spring day I attended a school athletics competition, arriving in the middle of the boys' 1,500-metre race. During the last lap of the race, the audience was on its feet cheering two boys who were running neck and neck for the final fifty metres. A short distance behind them ran a pack of four or five boys, jockeying for third place. The crowd broke into applause for the first and second place finishers, and then the crescendo grew again as the remaining pack fought for third place.

Another runner suddenly caught my attention, distracting me. As I looked down the track, I saw one boy lagging far behind. *Poor kid*. The portly first-year struggled for each breath, his face red and sweaty, the main artery in his neck bulging and throbbing to supply air to his oxygen-deprived lungs. Suddenly the woman to my left stepped over me and rushed down to the railing overlooking the track – she was obviously the boy's mother. She screamed, 'Johnny, *run faster!*'

I wish you could have seen the incredulous look on the little boy's face. He had to be thinking, 'Mum! *I'm running as fast as I can!*'

Spiritual growth does not happen by running faster.

What keeps many of us from growing is not sin, but speed.

Most of us are just like Johnny.

We are living life at a dizzying speed, and God is nowhere to be found. We're not rejecting God; we just don't have time for him. We've lost him in the blurred landscape as we rush by on our way to church. We don't struggle with the Bible, but with the clock. It's not that we're too decadent, we're too busy. We don't feel guilty because of sin, but because we have no time for our spouse, our children or our God. It's not sinning too much that's killing our souls, it's our schedule that's annihilating us. Most of us don't come home at night staggering drunk. Instead, we come home staggering tired, worn out, exhausted and drained because we live too fast.

Speed is not a sin, but neither is it neutral. Fast living used to mean a life of debauchery; now it just means fast – *but the consequences are even more serious.* Speeding through life endangers our relationships *and* our souls.

Voices surround us, always telling us to move faster. It may be our boss, our pastor, our parents, our wife, our husband, our politicians or, sadly, even ourselves. So we comply. We increase the speed. We live life in the fast lane because we have no slow lanes any more. *Every* lane is fast, and the only comfort our culture can offer is more lanes and increased speed limits. The result? Too many of us are running as fast as we can, and an alarming number of us are running much faster than we can sustain.

Speed damages our souls because living fast consumes every ounce of our energy. Speed has a deafening roar that drowns out the whispering voices of our souls and leaves Jesus as a diminishing speck in the rear view mirror of our lives.

Spiritual growth is not 'running faster', as in more meetings, more Bible studies and more prayer meetings. Spiritual growth happens when we slow our activity down, not when we increase it. If we want to meet Jesus, we can't do it on the run. If we want to stay on the road of faith, we have to hit the brakes, pull over to a rest area and stop. Christianity is not about inviting Jesus to speed through life with us; it's about noticing Jesus sitting at the rest stop.

While the church earnestly warns its congregation to watch for the devil, the devil is sitting in the congregation encouraging everyone to keep busy doing 'good things'. I've just received a letter from a woman minister who was on the edge of crashing and burning. She and her family joined a growing, active church, and quickly volunteered to help. But two years later, she realised that her entire family were speeding by each other in unrestrained zeal to lead one activity or another at church every week.

'*Run faster!*' this woman's church newsletter screamed, but the only way she could save her soul from death was to slow down, which meant finding a new job.

Sin does not always drive us to drink; more often it drives us to exhaustion. Tiredness is equally as debilitating as drunkenness. 'Burn-out' is slang for an *inner* tiredness, a fatigue of our souls. Jesus came to forgive us all our sins, including the sin of busyness. The problem with growth in the modern church is not the *slowness* of growth, but the *rushing* of growth.

He came to give us rest.

We know when we are ready for God to work in our lives when we're tired. When the weight of our lives begins to weigh us down, God is present in the heaviness. It turns out that weariness is next to godliness – because when our souls are tired we are able to hear his voice and, according to Matthew

11:31, what he's saying is, 'Come. Rest.'

The ugly truth, however, is that many of us *do not know how to rest!*

Actually, we do know how to rest, we simply refuse to choose rest. Rest is a decision we make. Rest is choosing to do nothing when we have too much to do, slowing down when we feel pressure to go faster, stopping instead of starting. Rest is listening to our weariness and responding to our tiredness, not to what is making us tired. Rest is the result of the humiliating recognition that we are not necessary. Rest is what happens when we say one simple word: 'No!' Rest is the ultimate humiliation, because in order to rest we must admit we are not necessary, that the world can get along without us, that God's work does not depend on us. Once we understand how unnecessary we are, only then might we find the right reasons to say yes. Only then might we find the right reasons to decide to be with Jesus instead of working for him. Only then might we have the courage to take a nap with Jesus.

Four non-principles of spiritual growth

What kind of spirituality comes from the ingredients we've just discussed? The messy kind, the unpredictable, unique, ordinary-follower-of-Christ kind. But there's more. I want to give you some important 'non-principles' of growth which are guaranteed to help you understand that there *are* no guarantees in the spiritual life, except for one: the longing for Jesus Christ is always underneath our every desire.

Non-principle 1: Spiritual growth encompasses a lifetime of decisions

We would all like to believe that growth results from one mighty decision, a 'once and for all' commitment to God. And while we should celebrate our initial decision to follow Christ, it's just the beginning of our spiritual journey, not the end. It represents the first of many decisions, all important, and all decisions that bring growth.

Hundreds – maybe even thousands – of decisions make up genuine growth, some moving us closer to God, some moving us further away, but all of them ultimately contributing to a deeper, richer and more textured relationship with God.

During my adolescence I made hundreds of decisions to become a Christian, to re-become a Christian, to re-dedicate my life to God, to re-dedicate my re-dedication, to go into full-time Christian service, to treat my parents better, to give God my hormones . . . I meant every one of those decisions, yet I only successfully acted on most of them for about two or three days. Still, those two or three days laid the groundwork for the next decision. I couldn't have made the next decision if I had not made the previous one. *I was growing one decision at a time.* No question about it, my growing looked inconsistent: two steps backward, one step forward, up and down, in and out, over and under. But I was growing, all the same.

Non-principle 2: Spiritual growth looks different for each of us

Growth – the frustrating and difficult attempt to find God's trail in the dusty terrain of our lives – can't be charted as a steadily climbing line. It goes up, down and sideways, giving it an irregular, jagged, odd shape. Genuine growth follows as many patterns are there are people. We uncover God's fingerprints in the dust of our busyness in a manner that's erratic, arbitrary, capricious, inconsistent, disjointed and irregular. In spite of all the growth gurus and experts out there, we can't clone, manipulate or systematise spiritual growth. We can't predict the unpredictable.

Most information about spiritual growth gives the impression that our spiritual lives should look like this:

But what if real spiritual growth looks more like this?

Usually when we analyse a graph like the one above, we make value judgments. The high spots represent the good or positive moments in our relationship with God while the low spots represent the bad or negative moments. But what would happen if we removed those kinds of value judgments from our thinking? What would happen if, in place of 'good' and 'bad', 'positive' and 'negative', 'high' and 'low', we used words like 'resting', 'listening', 'waiting', 'starting', 'returning', 'savouring', 'celebrating', 'dancing', 'learning', 'growing'? How would our understanding of the spiritual life be altered if we used these other words to describe our growing?

Maybe waiting is good and not waiting is bad. Maybe stopping has the same value as starting. Maybe success is bad and failure is good. Suddenly the ups and downs of spiritual growth come into better focus. Some of us grow fast; some slow; some both fast and slow.

Non-principle 3: Give God 60 per cent

For years I believed it when people told me, 'You either love God or you don't', 'You are either committed or you aren't', 'Give God 100 per cent!' Sounds very spiritual, but the truth is there is no such thing as 100 per cent commitment.

I am a morning person, so I wake up with a fairly high commitment level – say 73 per cent. Then I go to work and my commitment level drops to 45 per cent; I get a pay rise and my commitment level shoots up to 92 per cent; my wife and I have a row and it drops to 9 per cent; and then *Baywatch* comes on television and I'm up to 80 per cent again (just kidding). Every day my commitment level moves up and down like a boat in rough seas, and my overall commitment might average out to 57 per cent for the entire day. We *strive* for 100 per cent, we *want* to give 100 per cent (sometimes), we *wish* we could give 100 per cent, but life isn't quite so simple.

Dr Lorraine Monroe taught in a school in New York's Harlem for many years. In her advanced English class one year sat a very bright student who, until this particular year, had shown great promise. This year his marks suddenly nose-dived and he was obviously under-performing. Dr Monroe had a word with the boy, challenged him, threatened him, pleaded with him and counselled him. She tried everything, but he continued to float just above the fail line, at about 70 per cent. At the end of the school year, the young man barely passed, another casualty of the urban jungle.

Ten years later, Dr Monroe was walking to work one morning when a well-dressed young man approached her. 'Do you remember me?' he asked.

'Of course I do,' Dr Monroe replied, 'you were in my advanced English class many years ago. I remember you because you had so much talent and you wasted it in my class.'

'I know, Dr Monroe. I knew you believed in me, even though you were disappointed at my performance. I've always hoped I'd run into you again to thank you for believing in me, because I am one of the editorial writers for *Time* magazine now, and I owe much of my success to you. You see, Dr Monroe, my final year at school was a difficult year for my family. My father was in prison, my mother was a prostitute, my older brother was selling drugs, and I was left to care for my younger sister and brother. Dr Monroe, 70 per cent was 100 per cent of all I could give you!'[35]

Sometimes a 70 per cent commitment is 100 per cent of all we have to give. And God is there, in the middle of our 'meagre' 70 per cent, recognising the seeds of growth in what we're giving him. God will show up in whatever percentage we give him, which motivates us to give even more.

Non-principle 4: Reluctant growth is still growth

No matter how much we've grown, we still need to grow more. No matter how mature we are, we never stop maturing. And no matter how unspiritual we are, as long as we want to grow more, Jesus will show up in even the messiest of disciples. Take, for example, Daryl Jenkins.

Every month the youth group at River Road Church visited Holcomb Manor, a local nursing home, to hold church services for the residents. Daryl Jenkins was a reluctant adult helper at the youth group and did not like nursing homes. For a long time he had avoided the monthly services. But when a flu epidemic depleted the group of helpers, Daryl agreed to help with the next month's service as long as he did not have to do anything.

During the service, Daryl felt awkward and out of place. He leaned against the back wall, in between two residents in wheelchairs. Just as the service finished and Daryl was thinking about a quick exit, someone grabbed his hand. Startled, he looked down and saw a very old, frail and obviously lonely man in a wheelchair. What could Daryl do but hold the man's hand? The man's mouth hung open and his face held no expression. Daryl doubted whether he could hear or see anything.

As everyone began to go home, Daryl realised he didn't want to leave the old man. He had been left too many times in his own life. Caught somewhat off-guard by his feelings, Daryl leaned over and whispered, 'I'm . . . uh . . . sorry, I have to leave – *but I'll be back.* I promise.' Without any warning, the man squeezed Daryl's hand and then let go. Daryl's eyes filled with tears as he grabbed his stuff and started to leave. Inexplicably, he heard himself say to the old man, 'I love you.' (*Where did that come from? What's the matter with me?*)

Daryl returned the next month, and the month after that. Each time it was the same routine. Daryl would stand at the back, Oliver would grab his hand, Daryl would say he had to leave, Oliver would squeeze his hand, and Daryl would say softly, 'I love you, Mr Leak.' (He had learned his name, of course.) As the months went on, about a week before the Holcomb Manor service, Daryl would find himself looking forward to visiting his aged friend.

On Daryl's sixth visit, the service started but Oliver still hadn't been wheeled out. Daryl didn't feel too concerned at first because it often took the nurses a long time to wheel everyone out to the service. But halfway into the service Oliver still hadn't appeared and Daryl became alarmed. He went to the head nurse, 'Um, I don't see Mr Leak here today. Is he okay?' The nurse asked Daryl to follow her, and led him to Room 27.

Oliver lay in his bed, his eyes closed, his breathing uneven. At forty years of age Daryl had never seen someone dying, but he knew that Oliver was near death. Slowly he walked to the side of the bed and grabbed Oliver's hand. When Oliver didn't respond, tears filled Daryl's eyes. He knew he might never see Oliver alive again; he had so much he wanted to say, but the words wouldn't come out. He stayed with Oliver for about an hour, and then the youth director gently interrupted to say they were leaving.

Daryl got up to leave and squeezed Mr Leak's hand for the last time as he said, 'I'm sorry, Oliver, I have to go. I love you.' As he unclasped his hand, he felt a squeeze. Mr Leak had responded! He had squeezed Daryl's hand! The tears were unstoppable now, and Daryl stumbled towards the door, trying to gain his composure.

A young woman was standing at the door. Daryl

almost bumped into her. 'I'm sorry,' he said, 'I didn't see you.'

'It's all right, I've been waiting to see you,' she said. 'I'm Oliver's granddaughter. He's dying, you know.'

'Yes, I know.'

'I wanted to meet you,' she went on. 'When the doctors said he was dying, I came immediately. We have always been very close. They said he couldn't talk, but he's been talking to me. Not much, but I know what he is saying. Last night he woke up. His eyes were bright and alert. He looked straight into my eyes and said, "Please say goodbye to Jesus for me," and then he lay back down and closed his eyes. He caught me off-guard, and as soon as I gathered my composure I whispered to him, "Grandpa, you don't need to say goodbye to Jesus, you're going to be with him soon, and you can tell him hello." Grandpa struggled to open his eyes again. This time his face lit up with a mischievous smile and he said, as clearly as I'm talking to you, "I know, but Jesus comes to see me every month, and he might not know I've gone." He closed his eyes and hasn't spoken since.

'I told the nurse what he'd said, and she told me about you, coming every month, holding his hand. I wanted to thank you for him, for me . . . and, well, I never thought of Jesus as being as chubby and bald as you, but I imagine that Jesus is very glad to have had you mistaken for him. I know Oliver is. Thank you.'

She leaned over and kissed Daryl on the forehead.

Oliver Leak died peacefully the next morning.[36]

If a reluctant follower of Jesus like Daryl can be mistaken for Jesus, maybe you and I can as well.

7

Little Graces

The triumph of tiny living

Something is better than nothing.
Author unknown

*Just one person running loose in Southern California
who can say 'no' can cause a revival. You don't have to be
that good of a Christian to make other Christians. You
can just be a little Christian running around saying,
'No, we don't do that.'*
Will Willimon[37]

*One of the most insidious maladies of our time [is]: the
tendency in most of us to observe rather than act, avoid
rather than participate, not-do rather than do; the
tendency to give in to the sly, negative, cautionary voices
that constantly counsel us to be careful, to be controlled,
to be wary and prudent and hesitant and guarded in our
approach of this complicated thing called living.*
Arthur Gordon[38]

During the last months of World War II, the British conducted daily bombing raids over Berlin. The bombers would take off from an airstrip in England surrounded by smaller fighter planes whose job it was to keep German fighter planes from attacking the large targets of bombers.

One night after a successful bombing raid, as the bombers were heading for the safety of England, they were attacked by a large group of German fighter planes. Somehow, during the dogfights between fighters, one bomber crew found themselves flying alone with no protection, and suddenly a German fighter plane appeared out of nowhere. The crew of the bomber watched as the German plane moved closer and closer, until finally, it was in range. The bomber crew prepared for the worst and watched helplessly as tracer bullets began spitting from the German plane. They watched in horror as bullets whizzed by them, over and under, until thud! Thud! Thud! Thud! Thud! Five bullets slammed into the fuselage of the bomber in the location of the fuel tank. The moment they were hit the crew braced themselves for an explosion, but nothing happened. They could see fuel pouring from the holes the bullets had made, but there was no explosion. Miraculously they were able to make it back to their base and get safely off the plane.

A few hours after they landed, one of the mechanics showed up in the pilots' barracks. He had found five bullets inside the fuel tanks, crumpled but not exploded.

He handed the bullets to the pilots. They carefully opened the shells. To their amazement, they found each shell empty of gunpowder, and inside one of the shells they found, wrapped into a tiny wad, a ball of paper. When they unfolded the paper they found the following note:

> We are Polish POWs – forced to make bullets in factory. When guards do not look we do not fill with powder. Is not much, but is best we can do. Please tell family we are alive.

The note was signed by four Polish POWs.[39]

Five tiny bullets, out of millions and millions of bullets made during the war, and they made all the difference for the crewmen of a British bomber.

The power of goodness is found in the tiny. Since the beginning, God has chosen the tiny over the large – David and Goliath, Gideon and his 300 soldiers, Elijah over the prophets of Baal, one sheep over ninety-nine sheep . . . Spirituality is about doing the tiny work of God, little acts, small responses to God's presence in our lives. What my church shows me every week is all of the heroic acts accomplished by ordinary people who never will be recognised.

Because we have heard the biblical stories over and over again, we have enlarged the tiny ministry Jesus actually had. Yes, there were the crowds, but even when there were crowds he tried to avoid them, escape them, run from them. Jesus was around for three years, and he didn't do all that much. He hung out with a few guys, healed a leper or two and a couple of lame folk, made some wine, helped out three or four women, raised a few people from the dead, calmed down a crazy person or two, caused a scene in the temple, and then disappeared.

Think what Jesus could have accomplished if he'd stayed on earth for twenty, thirty or fifty more years. Wow, think what he could have done with all the technology available today!

Nope. Jesus showed up for a little while, did a few tiny miracles, said a few amazing words, and left.

But his few tiny acts changed the world for ever. Tiny becomes huge when Jesus is involved.

It is easy for us to get the impression that God is about big, spectacular and miraculous. After reading a few books, watching television, and listening to the stories at church, it is very easy to conclude that unless God is doing really big things through our lives, we're not spiritual.

Spiritual people are about tiny things, which is the fruit of their spirituality. The spiritual life is not a life of success, it is a life of faithfulness . . . and it's not easy. God does 'big' things once in a while, but there is also no question that the primary work of God in the world is salt and light tiny. God knew we would naturally be dazzled by big: that's why he told the parables of the lost sheep, the lost coin, the lost son, the mustard seed.

Jesus was trying to tell us something – the spiritual life is a tiny life, filled with little decisions, tiny steps towards God, tiny glimpses of his presence, little changes and small movings, tiny successes and imperceptible stirrings.

Stuck in the book of Mark is a four-verse story which is more like an aside than a significant event. (You can read it in Mark 12:41–4.) Jesus has just been ranting about excessive displays of arrogance and showy spirituality. He just finishes his rather heated criticism of those who want everyone to notice their piety, and he catches sight of a woman no one notices. Just by looking at her, Jesus recognises the unmistakable look of extreme poverty – clothes tattered, one ragged garment piled over another (she was cold, the elderly are always cold), stained with years of dirt. Shuffling across the temple grounds, she drops two thin coins in the temple collection box. Talk about an unimpressive moment! Old woman gives little gift. Nice story, but not the stuff movies are made of. As much as we would like to be moved over this woman's sacrifice, it doesn't come close to the life-threatening drama of the disciples and heroes of the faith.

Which is what makes the story of the widow powerful. It isn't powerful, dramatic, spectacular, revolutionary, significant or amazing. Here was a woman no one noticed and, worse, no one *cared* to notice her. In the world she lived in, she was part of the landscape, an anonymous blur in a crowd of faces, but she was a *faithful blur, an inconspicuous lover of God* who *loved* God every day and *lived* God every day. *She didn't care whether she was noticed*, she cared about whether *God* was noticed. Whether she understood or not, Jesus understood the power of people who couldn't care less about being noticed. Christianity shows itself most powerfully in the unnoticed life, in the inconspicuous servant, the unrecognised saint, the invisible disciple.

We shouldn't be surprised. Jesus chose not to change the world with armies, swords, legions of angels and lightning bolts. Instead, he changed the world by rejecting fame and welcoming the infamy of a criminal's death.

Tiny living is critical to our times because the media has an insatiable hunger for stories. Because we have so few heroes, we desperately need to create them. The stories I am about to tell are not to glamorise or make heroes out of people, but are to encourage all of us to recognise the power of the ordinary, the significance of the insignificant, the eternal difference that ordinary, messy, unfinished, under-construction people like you and me can make. Let me give you examples of tiny actions by a few inconspicuous, unnoticed disciples who have bought into the foolish, upside-down, invisible kingdom of God.

Michael: the boy who unchained his mother from depression

Michael's physical and mental disabilities required him to live in a twenty-four-hour care facility. His parents lived some distance away, and periodically Michael's mother suffered from bouts of depression brought on by guilt for not being able to care for her son. During one depressive episode she stayed in bed for days, unresponsive to all efforts to engage her, even her husband's. Concerned, Michael's father asked him to come home to see if his presence could bring her out of her deep despair.

Michael could walk but needed assistance with almost everything else, and his speech was impaired, making his words difficult to understand. When he arrived home, Michael walked straight into his mother's bedroom and sat on her bed. He stayed with her for a long time, but said nothing. When his father came into the bedroom, Michael pointed to a large flower vase and repeated over and over again, 'Ca . . . ca . . . ca . . . oke.' It took his father a while to understand that Michael was asking him to fill the vase with Coke.

When the father returned with the vase of Coke, Michael took a small piece of bread he had earlier found in the kitchen, then tenderly took hold of his mother's hand and placed the bread in it. He dipped the bread into the Coke and gently lifted the bread to his mother's mouth as he began stumbling through the words of communion. His mother's eyes filled with tears as she took the bread. Within a few hours she came out of her depression. Michael did what he could do, his mother's descent into depression stopped, and her recovery began.

Michael might not have been able to walk, but he

could *feel*! His speech might have been impaired, but his heart worked fine. His impromptu communion service might have seemed 'unbalanced' to some, but it's what helped his mother regain her balance. Michael had one gift even his father didn't have: *he knew what his mother needed*. Michael trusted what he could do instead of getting frustrated about what he couldn't do – and then he performed a tiny act of discipleship.

Michael could have lamented his limitations, he could have despaired about the impossibility of bringing his mother out of depression, he could have suggested his father hire a 'professional' to help his mother. Instead, he did what Christians do when they don't know what to do. He went to the arsenal of weapons which separate the Church from every other organisation, and decided on one of the most unlikely: communion. Michael realised that the foolishness of God is still more powerful than all the brilliant weapons of our culture. Just like a young girl named Lisa.

Lisa: the girl who made winners out of losers

Lisa (not her real name) decided to try out for the track athletics team in her rural high school. Her school had so few students that anyone who had a go at a sport got a place in the team. Aspiration rather than ability determined who would make the team.

Through sheer desire Lisa became the anchor runner

on the girls' 1,500-metre relay team. Because her school boasted the only girls' 1,500 relay team in its small league, Lisa and her running mates received an invitation to represent their league in the section finals. Everyone knew they had no chance to beat the more talented, experienced teams, yet before the race Lisa continually flashed a brilliant smile as if she were relaxed and enjoying herself.

Puzzled, a friend of mine asked Lisa why she was so calm. 'I love the relay!' she said. 'We're not very fast. I'm always the last one to finish, so when I come down the stretch the people in the stands cheer for me.'

Sure enough, during the final Lisa's team lagged far behind. As Lisa rounded the final turn, running hard for the finish line, everyone else had already left the track . . . but her smile lit up the course. The crowd was on its feet cheering as Lisa crossed the finish line.

'See,' Lisa later told my friend, 'we always get a standing ovation, and we're last. I love it.'

Lisa's my hero.

She has rejected the values of a culture that worships winning. She refuses to listen to those who say 'second is just the first to lose'. Lisa has decided that last can be as good as first. In her unknown corner of the world, she triumphs over those who would call her a 'loser'.

I am reminded of a small group of 'losers' who stood by the cross while Jesus died. Just a few days earlier thousands had cheered Jesus. Next thing you know, he's dying and alone, and a few of his friends decide they will stick with Jesus as he dies. I am also reminded of a list of 'unimpressive unknowns' in Romans chapter 16 (except that they *were* impressive). Listen to Paul's description of their heroic smallness:

- Phoebe: a servant of the church
- Priscilla and Aquila: church meets in their house
- Mary, Tryphena and Tryphosa, Persis: women who worked hard
- Andronicus and Junias: been in prison with me

Godly people, 'tested and approved in Christ', doing the tiny things Paul depended on for his survival. The Church was growing, spreading, adding thousands to its rolls every day, and yet Paul takes time to affirm and thank the people who had not forgotten him.

Like Claudio and Virgilio, street workers in Sao Paulo, Brazil.

Claudio and Virgilio: the boys who remembered one unremembered

One third of Brazil's 150 million inhabitants are under fourteen years of age. Twenty-five million children live in desperate poverty. Eight million are abandoned, needy and walk the streets. Thirty-five per cent of these boys and girls die on the streets before they reach the age of eighteen.

A group of us had come to Sao Paulo to see first-hand the tragedy of the street children of Brazil. We met Virgilio and Claudio, street kids themselves at one time, now giving their lives to reach the unreachable. As we walked towards a motorway underpass where many of the street children 'live' (if you can call it living), we found ourselves stranded on a cement island between four lanes of heavily travelled highway. Traffic sped by in both directions, making it impossible to cross the street.

Suddenly, in front of us we saw an emaciated young boy, sleeping on the cement island, using his hands as a pillow. How could someone sleep so soundly despite the noise and confusion of thousands of cars, the smothering heat and the unending commotion of the city, I asked Claudio. He told me the boy was sleeping off a crack high.

'Sometimes they can sleep for twenty-four hours, and you don't want to wake them,' Claudio warned, 'because the crack can make them very dangerous.'

I passed the boy, but when I turned back I saw Claudio bending down slowly, gently, touching him and speaking very softly: 'Andrew. Andrew.' He spoke with amazing compassion and care. The boy did not wake up and we kept walking.

Later Claudio told me the boy's story. Fourteen years old, Andrew was a crack addict who had once been involved in Claudio's rehabilitation project, but the lure of the street had proved too much.

That night as I sat in my room, thinking about Andrew

and Claudio and Virgilio, I could not stop the tears. Reaching eight million street kids is an overwhelming responsibility. Most of the eight million are like forgotten grains of sand. What's the point?

Claudio and Virgilio see it differently. Because of their ministry, only 7,999,999 grains are left – and one grain, Andrew, is not forgotten. Thank God for those who remember the forgotten! Thank God for two unknown men who have given their lives to saving one tiny grain of sand at a time.

Sue: the woman whose silence silenced the anger

A group of us were at a spiritual retreat when an innocent late-night discussion exploded into a toxic disagreement that escalated into an extremely angry argument. Provoked and frustrated, we all went to bed upset. The next morning we requested help from one of our spiritual directors, Sue, who graciously agreed to mediate the situation. Early in the afternoon we gathered in a small room and started unravelling the events of the night before. As the discussion went on, the tension in the room escalated and ugly words shot back and forth. Anger again filled the room. Meanwhile our spiritual director remained silent, making no attempt whatsoever to mediate. *What was the matter with her? Why wasn't she intervening?* Our discomfort increased, until our director's silence became so loud we stopped arguing. One by one we looked up to see Sue silently sobbing, her eyes reddened, her face distorted with anguish at our pain.

Without saying a word, our spiritual director broke through the anger in the room, silenced our shouting, connected with the deep cause of our bickering and put us on the road to reconciliation. Even though Sue did not understand the complicated, dysfunctional relationships among the members of our group, God used her silence and her tears to begin a process of healing.

Gertie: the old lady who infiltrated a youth group

At seventy-six years of age, Gertie Campbell became concerned about the young people in her church, so she volunteered to help with the school youth group.

'What would you like to do?' the pastor asked.

'I don't know,' she said, 'God and I will think of something.'

Gertie wasn't a speaker, she felt too old to play games and she didn't want to lead Bible studies or counsel at camp. But she had a camera, so she took pictures of every kid in the youth group, put a picture of each one on flash cards, and wrote some biographical information on the back of each. She memorised the picture and the information on each flash card, then stood at the door to the youth room each Sunday night. As the students entered, she welcomed each one by name. At the end of the meeting, Gertie stood at the door again, saying goodbye to each person by name, along with a promise to pray. Over the years, the church's young people discovered that Gertie had the Bible almost memorised, so they came to her with the questions and struggles of their young lives.

Ten years of youth ministry later, at eighty-six, Gertie suffered three strokes. The sad prospect of her possible death distressed all the kids in the youth group. They wanted to help her, to tell her how much she meant to them, but they didn't know how. One afternoon the youth leader had an idea.

'Gertie,' he told her, 'I want to do your funeral.'

'I know,' she said, '*I* want you to do my funeral – but I'm not dead yet.'

'Yes, but I want to do your funeral while you are *alive*, so that you can hear just how much you mean to our youth group and our church.'

Gertie loved the idea, and the youth group and its leader planned her living funeral.

As you might imagine, young men and women packed out the service. Many of them had graduated from college, married and had children of their own. Ten years' worth of students shared Gertie stories that night.

At the end of the evening, a group of young people gathered mysteriously at the back of the room. In order to understand what they were doing, you need to know something about Gertie. She may have been eighty-six, but she never lost her youth. No old-people's perfume for Gertie – she loved expensive designer perfumes. Estée Lauder's 'Beautiful' was her favourite.

The young people walked down the aisle, all clumped together in order to hide something. When they arrived at the front, they held up a giant, very expensive bottle of 'Beautiful' perfume, which they promptly broke and poured over Gertie's feet, anointing her feet in gratitude for all she had done. Like the widow, Gertie had given what she could. And like the widow with her tiny offering, Gertie's offering will live on long after she's gone.[40]

Michael, Lisa, Claudio and Virgilio, Sue and Gertie might not be recognised on the radar screen of the movers and shakers of the world. But God recognises them, and he recognises the other unrecognisables like you and me. Every tiny contribution we make to his kingdom is noticed and remembered, and one day we will understand just how beautiful our thin sacrifices have been.

Tiny mosaic

The town of Morehead, Minnesota, the home of Concordia College, lies in a very bleak part of the United States (especially during the winter). All year the community anticipates Concordia's annual Christmas concert. Each December, a huge choir and full orchestra give a musical performance in the concert hall at the college.

Every year the people in the community create a unique background for the concert – a hundred-foot by thirty-foot mosaic. Beginning in the summer, about six months before the concert, the community designs a new mosaic, rents an empty building, and the painting begins. Thousands of people, from primary school pupils to senior citizens, paint the mosaic. They paint by number on a very large-scale design that has thousands and thousands of tiny individual pieces. Day after day, month after month, one little painted piece at a time, the picture on the mosaic gradually comes into focus.

When everyone has finished painting, an artist goes over the entire creation, perfecting the final work of art. When the mosaic is completed, they place it behind the choir. It has the appearance of an enormous beautiful stained glass window. The weekend of the concert, those people who have helped paint arrive early, along with their friends and neighbours. Throughout the building you can hear people whispering, 'See that little green spot below the camel's foot? I painted it.'

Every year in the middle of summer in Morehead, Minnesota, thousands of unknown, ordinary people paint a tiny insignificant tile. Six months later, the result is a spectacularly beautiful masterpiece.

Our tiny choices and tiny moves towards God may not seem like much. But some day you and I will stand all together in the great cathedral of heaven, and up at the front, by Jesus, will hang the most magnificent mosaic we could ever imagine, made up of thousands and thousands of our tiny responses to God's love in our lives.

8

God's Annoying Love

The irresistibleness of grace

All the persons of faith I know are sinners, doubters,
uneven performers. We are secure not because we are sure
of ourselves but because we trust that God is sure of us.
Eugene Peterson[41]

'Does God like you,' I asked a five year old little girl.
She stifled a grin. She is a compassionate soul. 'Yep,' she
said easily, confidently, certainly. 'How do you know?'
'Because of the way he talks to me. He just likes me. I
recognize it in his voice.'

Robert Bensen[42]

I will not leave you alone. You are mine. I know each of
My sheep by name. You belong to Me. If you think I am
finished with you, if you think I am a small god that
you can keep at a safe distance, I will pounce upon you
like a roaring lion, tear you to pieces, rip you to shreds,

and break every bone in your body. Then I will mend
you, cradle you in my arms, and kill you tenderly.
Brennan Manning[43]

I had a paper round when I was eleven years old. It was one of the more difficult rounds, sprinkled with farms, rural homes and a smattering of hills. But the money was good, and my parents allowed me to keep my wages to buy the non-necessities of life (stereo, records, tape recorders, etc). Our family's lower-middle-class income had very little room for non-necessities. My monthly income forced me to learn about delayed gratification, savings accounts and other nuances of capitalism.

One ordinary Tuesday, while cruising the shops on my bicycle, I skidded to a halt as I passed a music store. There in the window, standing all by itself, was the most beautiful conga drum I had ever seen. It was almost as tall as me, and I could not take my eyes off its barrel-shaped beauty. Dark and light wood alternated around a laminated exterior, and a round chrome frame stretched the thick animal skin tightly over the top of the drum. It was 1953, and an eleven-year-old boy could not resist the allure of such a drum. Twenty dollars was a lot of money in those days, *but I had twenty dollars in my savings account.* Before the day was over, I had purchased a conga drum, brought it home and proudly showed it to all my friends. None of us knew how to play any kind of a drum, but it didn't stop us from pretending to be the most rhythmically talented group of boys in the world.

And then my father arrived home from work. Anxious

to show him my new purchase, I pranced into the kitchen beating on my drum as loudly as I could, beaming from ear to ear.

'Where did you get that?' my dad said sharply.

I hesitated, 'Uh, I bought it with my paper round money, Dad. It's a conga drum! Isn't it beautiful?' I was very proud.

'How much did you pay for it?' His harshness continued.

'Twenty dollars,' I said meekly, still waiting for him to share my excitement and joy over the conga drum.

'Twenty dollars????' I was not prepared for his anger. I stood there stupidly while my new drum slowly slid from my side on to the kitchen floor. Nothing but silence, and then the words I shall never forget, 'Take it back!'

I couldn't believe what I was hearing. My parents had emphasised over and over again that my paper round money was mine. As long as I didn't spend the money on something illegal or immoral, I was free to buy what I wanted. I wanted the conga drum, and my father was ordering me to take it back. (My father had grown up during the Great Depression. In fairness to him, he thought the music shop assistant had taken advantage of an eleven-year-old boy. Of course, I didn't understand this at the time.)

The next morning I took the drum back. For reasons I don't really understand to this day, the trauma of that experience burned itself deep into my soul. Emotionally I was crushed, and every good experience since has been shadowed by the fear of hearing the words 'Take it back.' Buried in the back of my mind is gnawing worry that my grace credit card is going to be cancelled. Parked somewhere in my sub-conscious is the belief that grace and forgiveness are lavish, unconditional and ... *limited*.

Cross Jesus one too many times, fail too often, sin too much, and God decides to take his love back. It is so bizarre, because I know Christ loves me, but I'm not sure he likes me and I continually worry that God's love will simply wear out. Periodically I have to be slapped in the face with Paul's words in Romans:

> I am convinced that neither death, nor life, neither angels nor demons, neither the present nor the future, nor any powers, neither height nor depth, nor anything else in all creation, *will be able to separate us from the love of God that is in Christ Jesus our Lord.*
>
> Romans 8:38

God's love is sticky

Lots of religious-sounding words, but the bottom line is that we are all stuck with God's love whether we want to be or not. The words 'nor anything else in all creation' mean *nothing* can stop God from loving us. Nothing. He just keeps loving us. In modern language you could say, 'neither failure, poor church attendance, inadequate Bible reading and prayer, betrayal, denial, doubt, insecurity, guilt, weakness, bad theology nor even losing our temper can separate us from the love of God'. He loves us when we don't want him to love us. He loves us when we don't act like a Christian. He loves us when our lives are a mess. His love is sticky, resistant to rejection, aggressive and persistent. The challenge is on, so go ahead – resist his love, run from it, hide from it. Go ahead and try.

In the film *The Great Santini*, 'Bull' Meechum (Robert Duvall) is a US Marine father who cannot leave his military training at home. His children (he calls them 'hogs', just like new recruits) are awakened early every morning and ordered to stand in line for 'inspection'. Yet despite the fact that he's as blustery and difficult as he is, Duvall's four children love and respect their father. Children can tell when they are loved, and although Daddy has a tough exterior they know he loves them. But Daddy, like every daddy, has his share of flaws.

All his life Bull Meechum has been fighting the demons of his childhood with a father who was never satisfied, always demanding more from his son. Bull and his oldest son, Ben, have a very close relationship which begins to fall apart as the son matures.

Late one evening, Duvall staggers into his house drunk, and begins to beat up his wife. Hearing the mother's screams, the children jump out of their beds, race down the stairs and attempt to restrain their father. Ben grabs his father by the collar and throws him against the wall while the other three children try to grab his legs and arms. When the screaming and crying die down, Bull stumbles backwards and drunkenly realises he has come to the edge of destroying his marriage and his family. Humiliated, angry and mostly incoherent, Bull Meechum backs away from his family and storms outside.

Later, after the children are quietened down and in bed, Ben finds his mother standing on the porch. 'I'm getting worried,' she says, 'your father may be in trouble.'

'Good,' Ben snaps back, 'I hope he dies.'

'No, you don't,' the mother protests. 'I want you to go and get him.'

Ben reluctantly searches for his father in the empty streets near their house. At last he thinks he hears his voice, and turns to find Bull Meechum slumped against a tree mumbling a sad imaginary dialogue with his own father. As the son listens to his father's tearful words, he begins to understand why his dad is the way he is. Finally, his dad falls down on the grass, crying, and Ben stoops to pick him up. 'Come on, Dad, let's go home. I think I understand now.'

As he picks up his father he gently says, 'I love you, Dad.' His father pushes Ben away and staggers across the park. Ben, angry at first, keeps saying, 'I love you, Dad. I love you.' Bull tries to escape his son, but Ben starts circling his dad, taunting him, 'I love you, Dad. Come on, Dad, I love you! Stop me, Dad, come on, stop me! I love you, Dad.' Finally, when it becomes clear to his father that he cannot escape or run away from his son's love, Ben picks up his father and helps him home.

Bull is angered by his son's unconditional, relentless,

stubborn love. He doesn't deserve his son's love and he knows it. He has been a flawed, bullheaded father. He has failed many times, too many. He tries to drown out his son's words, but he can't.

That love was infuriating. No matter how ugly Bull became, his son refused to stop loving him. Ben reminds us of a God who refuses to stop loving us no matter what mess we've made of our lives. He refuses to exclude us. That is why he finally had to send us Jesus.

Until Jesus came along, we were all outside the fence of God's grace.

In the Second World War, a group of American soldiers were fighting in the rural countryside of France. One rainy night, during an intense battle, one of the American soldiers was killed. His comrades did not want to leave his body on the battlefield and decided to give him a Christian burial. A few miles behind the front lines, they remembered a church whose grounds included a small cemetery surrounded by a white fence. After receiving permission to take their friend's body to the church cemetery, they arrived just before sunset.

A priest, his bent back and frail body betraying his many years, responded to their knocking. His face, deeply wrinkled and tanned, was the home of two fierce eyes that flashed with wisdom and passion.

'Our friend was killed last night, and we wanted to give him a church burial,' the soldiers blurted out.

Apparently the priest understood what they were asking, although he spoke in very broken English. 'I'm sorry,' he said, 'but we can only bury those of the same faith here.'

Weary after many months of war, the soldiers simply turned to walk away.

'But,' the old priest yelled, 'you can bury him outside the fence.'

Cynical and exhausted, the soldiers dug a grave and buried their friend just outside the white fence. They finished after nightfall.

The next morning the entire unit was ordered to move on, and the group of Americans raced back to the little church for one final goodbye to their friend. When they arrived they couldn't find the grave site. Tired and confused, they knocked on the door of the church and immediately recognised the old priest. They asked if he knew where they had buried their friend, 'It was dark last night and we were exhausted. We must have been disoriented.'

A smile flashed across the old priest's face. 'After you left last night, I could not sleep, so I went outside early this morning and *I moved the fence*.'[44]

Jesus did more than move the fence – he tore it down. No wonder he made the scribes and Pharisees nervous; fence-makers do not like their fences torn down.

God's grace is unfair

Jesus told a parable which by anyone's standards is offensive, discriminatory, elitist, ridiculous and very annoying (it's in Matthew 20:1–16). Early in the morning a wealthy landowner hires some unemployed men to work his vineyard at an agreed price (one denarius). As the day progresses he hires more workers, promising to pay them fairly. He hires workers at 9 a.m., noon, 3 a.m. and as late as five o'clock in the afternoon. At the end of the day, the foreman, as per the landowner's instructions, pays the workers in order, starting with the last ones who were hired. The latecomers who worked only an hour or so received one denarius. Those who worked longer, therefore, reasoned that if the people who worked little more than an hour received one denarius, they would, of course, receive more. But they didn't. Everyone received one denarius *no matter how long they worked*. If this story were to take place today, the landowner would be sued, and he would lose. Given the level of anger and rage in today's world, he would probably be physically assaulted or experience some kind of vengeful property damage. Who could blame the perpetrators? Who of us would not have sympathy for a person who worked eight hours and received only as much as a person who worked one hour? It's not fair.

Let's be honest, this story is out of place and out of touch with the modern world, or with any democratic society for that matter. Civilised people do not behave this way. We believe in equality, fairness and the right to be paid equitably. We have laws to protect us from arbitrary, capricious, unfair employers. What is even more disturbing is Jesus' explanation of the parable. He says '*the kingdom of God is like this'*! What? Wait a minute. If there is one eternal constant, one attribute of God we can trust unequivocally, it is God's fairness. God is the eternal monitor of fairness, isn't he? Life may not be fair, but God is definitely fair, right?

Not according to this parable. Generous? Yes. Fair? No. We should have known. Jesus gives us plenty of warning. The last will be first. You have to die to live. Clearly Jesus' love is more than radical, it is arbitrary, bewildering, shocking and offensive. None of us wants to admit it, but if we had started work at sunrise we would have resented those who only worked an hour and received the same pay. Loving everyone is a great concept, but when love contradicts our sense of fairness we are angry. Yes, we're all in favour of God's love, but he can't love one person more than another, can he? God simply can't forgive you more than he forgives me, can he? Whether we want to admit it or not, buried deeply into our notion of God's love is fairness. If God's love is unfair, then it is far more offensive and far more mysterious than we could ever have imagined. Yet God's 'unfairness' was great news to those who were unemployed with no hope of being hired. His love may be 'unfair', but when his 'unfairness' includes you and me . . . who wants to argue?

There are many examples of God's unfair love in the Bible. The prodigal son, Zacchaeus the tax collector and the woman caught in adultery qualify – but the most outrageous example is the thief on the cross.

No more chances for the thief. No more appeals. No last-minute legal manoeuvres. No possibility of rescue or a miracle. Luke tells us the thief knew he was guilty and knew he was getting what he deserved. The law was fair. This man had violated the law and now he had to pay. The thief was being treated fairly, and even he couldn't argue. But there, next to him, was Jesus. He was not being treated fairly. Everyone understood what was really going on, that his death penalty was all about power and politics. Even a thief knows innocence when he sees it. Even a thief knows the difference between fair and unfair. But the heart cannot always remain silent. Sometimes the longings which live there force their way into our voice. The thief blurts out to Jesus, 'Remember me when you come into your kingdom.' Can you imagine what he must have been thinking?

Oh my God! What did I just say? What is the matter with me? I'm lost, man, I'm finished. My life is over. My luck finally ran out. I don't even know this guy next to me except . . . I feel as if I do. Innocence reeks from his torn body. And his eyes, they see right through me. The attraction to him is unbearable, I can't stop looking at him! What did I say, again? Oh yeah, 'Remember me!' I don't believe I said that. Why would he remember me? What would innocence have to do with someone as contaminated as me? This makes no sense whatsoever. I deserve what is happening to me, but here I am asking him to take me with him to wherever it is he's going. This is crazy! Some people say this Jesus dude is God, and if he is then I'm done for. One thing I learned at synagogue, God is just. God is fair. Wait a minute, he's mumbling something. I . . . I . . . can't quite understand.

'I tell you the truth, today you will be with me in paradise.'

How unfair! Shouldn't the thief have been asked to repent, to make amends, at least to declare that he was sorry? No lectures, no sermons, no teaching or demands for repentance, Jesus just ushers the man into the kingdom of God. Shouldn't we be more careful with the requirements for receiving grace? Apparently not.

God's love is persistent

A young man and his wife had been trying to have a child for five years and had exhausted all their options. Childlessness began to hammer away at both of them. Difficult questions consumed them. How could two healthy lovers of God find themselves childless while so many women who never thought about God were having unwanted babies left, right and centre?

Five years of God's silence began to take its toll – and then the miracle happened. The man's wife became pregnant! Within a few months the news got even better: she was carrying twins.

The landscape of the couple's faith changed radically. Gone were their questions. God was good and God was visible. Now the five years of waiting made sense! God had been teaching them to wait, and now was giving them more than they had asked for. Life was good. Life made sense!

Then the unravelling began.

During a routine check-up, the doctors discovered serious pregnancy problems. One of the babies had already died; the other had little chance of surviving. If it did live, it would probably suffer severe disabilities. Abortion was the only way out, the doctors said.

The bottom dropped out of my friend's life. He felt devastated, angry, frustrated, hurt, confused and hopelessly lost in his grief. How could God do this? What kind of a God gives you a gift then takes the gift from you and destroys it? My friend was hanging on to his faith by a thin piece of thread. In fact, he would say later that his faith was hanging on to him. *He* had long since let go.

Friends at his church noted his deep exhaustion and strongly encouraged him to try and pick up the pieces of his life. He accompanied me on a week of silent retreat, but he made it clear he did not want to be there and didn't try to hide his anger.

One of the spiritual exercises during the retreat was a nature walk. The spiritual director instructed us to look for places in nature where we could see God. It made my friend furious.

'This is stupid,' he said. 'As far as I'm concerned, God is not anywhere. I am not going to waste an hour trying to find God in nature. I have been wasting the last few months trying to find God in my life, and I have received no response.'

He made up his mind that he would refuse to participate in the nature walk. He would walk, all right, he would *look* as if he was participating; but he would sabotage the experience by finding a long concrete path where he would walk, gazing only at the concrete. He would not look at any natural plants. He would spend an hour in quiet rebellion, staring at the bleak, smooth concrete.

After the exercise he returned to his small group to describe what happened.

'I was about halfway along the path,' he said, 'walking very slowly, lost in my anger and resentment of God, when the tears began. I was not conscious of my tears until my mind caught up with my heart. There were cracks in the concrete. The entire walkway was covered with cracks. I realised my tears were not because of the cracks, they were caused by what was *in* the cracks – in *every* crack, a flower! Somehow, in the midst of the grey lifeless concrete, *life made its way through the impenetrable rock and mortar of the pavement!* Suddenly I was conscious of God. He was alive! He surprised me with his flowers. He found a way to show me hope in the midst of despair. His love and care had found me.'

Somehow, in the ruins of a man's life, while anger and rage swirled all around with his life in a shambles, while he languished in despair – even while he was rejecting God – *God kept the conversation going.* God chased my friend into his arms.

The annoying conga drum

Recently I was at a spiritual retreat with my oldest son, and the conga drum experience resurfaced. Late one evening in the middle of the retreat, I told the story to my son for the first time. The scar on my soul still remained. On the final day of the retreat, just before communion, I led a short devotional session. Although I had prepared a few notes the talk was mostly spontaneous, and the story of the conga drum spilled out of me as an illustration of something I was talking about. Neither my son nor I had expected the story to be told.

When I finished, I sat down to prepare for communion. The hushed and silent chapel reflected our anticipation of the sacrament. The long silence continued. Then, without warning, my son marched to the front of the chapel, making an unusual amount of noise. He certainly grabbed everyone's attention. After loudly stamping up the stairs to the platform, he disappeared behind a large oak podium and started rustling through papers and cardboard, searching for something. Suddenly he turned to face the audience, holding in his hands a large shiny new conga drum. He moved forward, placing the conga drum on the altar.

Tears filled my eyes as I sat there, stunned. *Is this for me? Can I keep the conga drum?* The logic in me insisted that although this was a beautiful gesture from my son, it really wasn't mine to keep. *How can it be? He didn't have any idea I was going to talk about the drum. I know, he must have remembered a conga drum in the storage room backstage and spontaneously decided it would be a great way to close the service.* Clearly it was not mine to keep, so I did not reach for the drum. I wasn't about to have to give it back again.

I will never forget what happened next. From the back of the room I heard the words, 'Take the conga drum!' Slowly I rose and came to the altar, staring through tears at the most beautiful conga drum I had ever seen. I did not pick it up – I flung my arms around it and hugged it off the altar. My son told me later he was going to tell the story and present me with the drum, but when I started telling the story he realised God had orchestrated the morning far beyond anyone's expectations.

On top of the bookcase behind me sits a conga drum. Forty-seven years is a long time to wait, but the waiting is over. Each time I look at it, my heart laughs at a God who conspired to make sure I understood for ever his fathomless grace. Every day I hear him whisper, 'I'll never take back my grace!' I hope you hear him whispering, too.

Epilogue

I was returning home from a church retreat in some faraway town and had spent three sessions pleading with the congregation to bring their busy, lopsided lives to Jesus. As soon as the last meeting was over I raced to the airport to catch a plane home. Unfortunately my plane was delayed and by the time I reached San Francisco I had missed my connection and it was hours before the next available flight. I collapsed emotionally. I was stuck inside the walls of a crowded, noisy airport and I wanted to be home with my wife. I was imprisoned by guilt for abandoning her, for taking on too many speaking engagements – you name it, I felt guilty about it. I was depressed and angry and didn't have the spiritual resources to deal with it. Then it occurred to me that my son and daughter-in-law lived just a few miles away from the airport. I could phone them and talk to my grandson. 'Talking with him is guaranteed to cheer me up,' I thought.

'Hello, Noah,' I said.

'Ih habon ith dada,' the little voice mumbled. Life is cruel. Children just learning how to speak should not be talking to fifty-six-year-olds who are losing their hearing (at my age little children's voices are the voices I most need to hear).

I decided to use the tried-and-tested grandparent trick . . . go with phonics and fake it. 'You are playing with Dada?' It worked.

'Dada! Pluh da twain!'

'You're playing with your train?' I'm on a roll.

'Tain! Tain! Muffo grotos!'

Muffo grotos? I was desperate now. 'Mummy is there, too?'

'No. No. *Muffo grotos!*' The two-year-old equivalent of 'Can't you understand English?'

There is no hope now. Not only am I delayed from getting home, I am an inadequate grandfather who is incapable of hearing his own grandson. My gloomy disposition had now become even blacker. There was only one way out: 'Let me talk to Daddy, Noah!'

There was a long silence. My frustration was building. 'Great! Noah is not searching for Daddy, Noah has abandoned the telephone and is playing with his train. I am stuck in this airport and the telephone is lying on the floor! Who knows how long it will lie there!' Now I was frustrated *and* furious! I would wait one more minute and then I would hang up! But as I was about to put the phone down a tiny voice spoke as clearly as any voice I have ever heard. 'I love you, Grandpa!'

My eyes filled with tears and they would not stop. My gloom disappeared. My frustrations vanished. The darkness receded and light filled my soul. My grandson had spoken the only words my too busy life needed to hear. With four tiny words my grandson helped me put into perspective my delayed flight, my bad hearing, my increasing anxiety and my lopsided schedule. 'I love you, Grandpa' was all I needed to hear.

Life is complicated. Our schedules are hectic. Following Jesus is not always easy, nor is he easy to hear in the noisiness of our lives. Religion can be hard on our bones. My fervent prayer is that throughout this book you heard the crystal-clear voice of Jesus whispering, 'I love you.' May you hear him in your unfinishedness, your incompleteness, your incompetence – in other words, in your particular mess. He's there, you know.

Notes

1 As quoted by William McNamara in *Run with the Horses* by Eugene Peterson (InterVarsityPress, USA, 1983), p. 9.

2 *Children's Letters to God,* edited by Stuart Hample and Eric Marshall (Workman Publishing, USA, 1991).

3 Robert Coles in an interview with the *Wittenburg Door* (Issue No. 107, September/October 1989), pp. 17–18.

4 Anne Lamott, *Traveling Mercies* (Pantheon Books, USA, 1999), pp. 49–50.

5 Eugene Peterson, *A Long Obedience in the Same Direction* (InterVarsityPress, USA, 1980), p. 49.

6   Walter Wangerin, *Ragman and Other Cries of Faith* (Harper and Row, USA, 1984), p. 6.

7   Keith Miller as quoted in *The Problem of Wineskins* by Howard Snyder (InterVarsityPress, USA, 1975), p. 90.

8   Henri Nouwen as quoted in *Disciplines for the Inner Life* (Word, USA, 1985), p. 30.

9   Barbara Brown Taylor, *The Preaching Life* (Cowley Publications, USA, 1993), pp. 110–12.

10 Ron Lee Davis, *A Forgiving God in an Unforgiving World* (Harvest House, USA, 1984), p. 63.

11 Quoted from Nelson Mandela's 1994 Inaugural Speech.

12 From Donna Maclean, *All I Need to Know about Life I Learned from My Bible*, copyright 2001. Used with permission.

13 Parker Palmer, *Let Your Life Speak* (Jossey-Bass, USA, 2000), p. 34.

14 From Shel Silverstein, *Where the Sidewalk Ends* (Harper and Row, USA, 1974), p. 153. Used with permission.

15 Don McCullough, *The Trivialization of God* (NavPress, USA, 1995), p. 37.

16 Brennan Manning, *Lion and Lamb* (Chosen Books, USA, 1986), pp. 172–3.

17 Ron Lee Davis, *Mistreated* (Multnomah, USA, 1989), pp. 85–6.

18 A.W. Tozer, *The Knowledge of the Holy* (Harper and Row, USA, 1961), p. 63.

19 Mary Chapin Carpenter, 'Jubilee'.

20 Mike Riddell, *Alternative Spirituality for the Third Millennium* (Lion Publishing, UK, 1997), pp. 135–9.

21 Rich Wilkerson, *Straight Answers to Tough Questions about Sex* (Whitaker House, USA, 1987), pp. 213–17.

22 Parker Palmer, *Let Your Life Speak* (Jossey-Bass, USA, 2000), p. 4.

23 Kathleen Norris, *The Cloister Walk* (Riverhead Books, USA, 1996), p. 39.

24 Walker Percy as quoted in *Harvard Diary* by Robert Coles (Crossroad, USA, 1988), p. 26.

25 Henri Nouwen, *The Inner Voice of Love* (Doubleday, USA, 1996), p. 89.

26 Robert Fulghum, *Uh-Oh* (Villard Books, USA, 1991), pp. 35–8.

27 C.S. Lewis, *The Lion, the Witch, and the Wardrobe* (Collier Books, USA, 1950), p. 137.

28 Ibid., p. 37.

29 Dan Taylor, *Letters to My Children* (InterVarsityPress, USA, 1989), pp. 13–17.

30 *Children's Letters to God,* edited by Stuart Hample and Eric Marshall (Workman Publishing, USA, 1991).

31 Robert Capon, *Between Noon and Three* (Harper and Row, USA, 1982), p. 148.

32 Jacques Ellul, *The Presence of the Kingdom* (Seabury Press, USA, 1967), p. 69.

33 Sue Monk Kidd, *When the Heart Waits* (Harper and Row, USA, 1990), p. 152.

34 Doug Webster, *The Easy Yoke* (NavPress, USA, 1995), pp. 136–7.

35 As told in Dr Monroe's lecture at the Youth Specialties 1994 National Youth Workers' Convention.

36 Not an actual story, but a composite of many nursing home experiences during my tenure as pastor.

37 Will Willimon in an interview in the *Wittenburg Door* (Issue No. 129, May/June 1993); p. 8.

38 Arthur Gordon, *A Touch of Wonder* (Jove Books, USA, 1974), p. 161.

39 *Illustrations*, compiled by Wayne Rice (Youth Specialties/Zondervan, 2001).

40 Told to me by Brewster McLeod, Lexington, Kentucky.

41 Eugene Peterson, *A Long Obedience in the Same Direction* (InterVarsityPress, USA, 1980), p. 86.

42 Robert Bensen, *Between the Dreaming and the Coming True* (HarperSanFrancisco, USA, 1996), p. 49.

43 Brennan Manning, *Lion and Lamb* (Chosen Books, USA, 1986), p. 129.

44 William Barclay, *The Daily Study Bible* (Westminster Press, USA, 1954), p. 135.